IMAGES
of America

THE NEW YORK CITY
TRIANGLE FACTORY FIRE

Fire hoses sprayed water into the Asch Building (now known as the Brown Building). It only took 20 minutes to put out the fire that had engulfed the Triangle Waist Company on the eighth, ninth, and 10th floors. But by then, 146 people had died horribly. (Workers United.)

ON THE COVER: On April 5, 1911, four-hundred thousand people walked in or watched the "Trade Parade," organized by 60 trade unions, for seven unidentified victims of the Triangle fire. Horses draped with black netting pulled an empty hearse decked with flowers. Marchers walked silently in a steady downpour. (Library of Congress.)

IMAGES
of America

THE NEW YORK CITY TRIANGLE FACTORY FIRE

Leigh Benin, Rob Linné, Adrienne Sosin,
and Joel Sosinsky with Workers United
(ILGWU) and HBO Documentary Films

ARCADIA
PUBLISHING

Published by Arcadia Publishing
Charleston, South Carolina

Library of Congress Control Number: 2010931929

For all general information, please contact Arcadia Publishing:
Telephone 843-853-2070
Fax 843-853-0044
E-mail sales@arcadiapublishing.com
For customer service and orders:
Toll-Free 1-888-313-2665

Visit us on the Internet at www.arcadiapublishing.com

This book is dedicated to Rose Oringer and all the victims of the Triangle fire. In the Report of the Joint Relief Committee of the Ladies' Waist and Dressmakers Union No. 25, International Ladies Garment Workers Union (ILGWU) on the Triangle fire disaster, entry 46 begins: "R. O., 19 years old, earned $10 a week, union member, killed." At the time of her death, beautiful, vivacious Rose was engaged to be married. (Philip Maier.)

CONTENTS

LETTER TO A DEAD GREAT-AUNT

This letter was originally published on www.wowowow.com by Shelia Nevins in July 2008.

Great-Aunt Celia
Mount Zion Cemetery: Section 43
Queens, New York

Dear Great-Aunt Celia,

It is nearly 100 years since your tragic death in the Triangle Shirtwaist Factory Fire on March 25, 1911, but it is just today that I discovered you really existed and that your death in the fire was real. It hit me hard and I cried for you; and yet I never met you. I had heard that Grandma Fanny's youngest sister had died at the Triangle Fire, yet it always seemed like family folklore—and, anyway, my father was born some three years later. Occasionally your death would come up in family conversations, but I am sorry to say, only briefly, and Grandma Fanny's eyes would tear up and then we would go on to fresh borscht or stuffed cabbage and some relative from the other side would try to coax me to try some sweet and sour Russian food that I had no interest in. So here I am working on a documentary, called *Schmatta*, on a Friday in the year 2008. The film is about the fall of the garment center as a microcosmic look at the fall of Industrial America. The producer mentioned immigrant labor and *the fire*. I say, "I think I had a great-aunt who died in it."

"Really," he said.

"Yes," I said.

"Well, there is a list of all who died," he said.

"Oh," I say, "but I don't know my grandmother's maiden name. She was born in Russia and she married my grandfather there. I'll ask my Uncle Seymour." I say, "My father is dead. Uncle Seymour is my grandmother's only living child."

"Uncle Seymour," I ask later that night. "Did you know Grandma Fanny's maiden name?"

"Gitlin," he says without hesitation.

"G-I-T-T-L-I-N," I spell.

"No, one T."

"And what was her dead sister's name, the one who died in the fire?"

"I don't know," Uncle Seymour says, "but my name was supposed to be like hers."

Uncle Seymour is sharp as a tack at 84; he says his grief-stricken mother left the United States several months later to go to Belarus because she had to tell her mother, Lypska, that her youngest daughter was dead. There were only telegraph wires then, Grandma only spoke Yiddish, and no one in the Western Union telegraph office understood how to write it. Anyway, she thought her mother would die if she was alone when she found out Celia was dead. So, Grandma Fanny would take the nine day trip back to Russia. My uncle said she didn't know she was two-months pregnant with my father. Neighbors on the Lower East Side had gathered money for her trip and

6

she gave birth to my father in Russia. She stayed with her mother for two years before returning to America. Pogroms had broken out in Belarus and Grandma Fanny and her newborn son hid in her mother Lypska's grocery store basement for two years. For reasons Uncle Seymour didn't know, his grandmother died during her daughter Fanny's stay. Maybe it was grief over your death that killed your mother. Who knows? That's the history, Celia, your history as best we can tell it—your mother mourned you. The newspapers listed you as Celina Gitlin, but we knew at the morgue, it was our Celia Gitlin. On the death certificate it was correct—Celia from Clinton Street. You spoke no English. Neither did anyone in the family. Immigrants' names were up for grabs.

Dear Aunt Celia, you died at 17. The fire was on the 25th of March. Did you lay there suffering on Greene Street? Did you die immediately and your corpse lay alone on the curb? The death notice said your skull was fractured. Did you jump? Of course your sister Fanny got you the job at the shirt factory in America. She summoned you from Russia and said that you could be rich some day and meet a good man in America. She said you could share their one room apartment at 174 Clinton Street until your prince came to save you. There was plenty of room for you there—it was a big room. The bathtub was in the kitchen but don't worry, it had a curtain for privacy.

You came alone on a ship in early July 1910. You brought a samovar and a small sewing machine. I have the samovar. It wound up with me. I never asked where it came from. Now I know. I wish I could have met you at Ellis Island. If only for a moment, for you died eight months later—that's what it says on your death certificate. I wasn't alive then either or I would have been there. Aunt Celia, did you try the doors? Were you trampled by other women? Did you jump from the window because the exit doors were locked so the working girls couldn't smoke? Did you smoke? You were just a little girl. Who taught you to sew? I'm left-handed and terrible at sewing. Do I look like you? Did you think any of the thoughts I thought at seventeen? What did you pack for lunch that day? Could you ever forgive your sister, my Grandma Fanny, for bringing you to America? Did you walk to work that day? A 16-hour workday. A 7-day workweek. Were you tired that Saturday or did you think you were lucky to have a job in this shirt sweatshop? Would you have liked me, Celia? I want to know. And I want you to know how sad I am that you died so young. Did you ever know love? You were certainly beloved. Was it scary alone on the boat to America? Did the sewing machine and samovar smell of Old Russia? Were you proud to go to your new job? Did you audition for the Triangle boss with your Russian sewing machine? Celia, I mourn for you, for the lack of safety and the treatment of immigrants because I am one. I am outraged and panic when a crane kills a worker, or there is a senseless fire in a nightclub, or an immigrant is ruthlessly deported, for I am the child of immigrants—your grand niece. My father was born in Russia. Celia, I think I see the ghost of you. I see the babushka pulling back your kinky long hair so that it won't be caught in the sewing machine. Uncle Seymour's name is like yours, Uncle Sey-mour, Ce-lia. We feel you, Celia, in our hearts as a relative who owns a piece of our being. Sheila-Celia.

I will visit your grave at Mount Zion Cemetery and place a stone for you from all of us. I'm not religious, but I believe in remembering. I want to tell you how sorry I am that you lost your life. My heart aches for you and all the young immigrant girls who lost their lives for greed on that day in March . . . March 25, 1911, The Triangle Shirtwaist Factory Fire.

May all of you rest in peace.

With all my love,
In Memory,
Fondest,
Your Grandniece Sheila

ACKNOWLEDGMENTS

This book would not have been possible without the invaluable assistance of many supportive people. We would like to thank as many of them here as possible: Edgar Romney and Sherry Kane, Workers United; Daphne Pinkerson, Marc Levin, Michael Hirsch, and Justin Sirizzotti, Blowback Productions; Sheila Nevins, HBO Documentary Films; Barbara L. Morley, Kheel Center, Cornell University; Jane Ashdown, Adelphi University; Ruth Sergel and the members of the Remember the Triangle Fire Coalition; Metropolitan Klezmer; Michael Nash, Tamiment Library; Damon Compagna, NYC Fire Museum; Robert Domingo, FDNY; Hanna Griff, Eldridge Street Synagogue Museum; The Frances Perkins Center; Michael Sosin; Philip Maier; Diane Fortuna; Suzanne Pred Bass; Susan Blanc Harris; Lulu Lolo; the Steinberg family; and Erin Vosgien, Arcadia Publishing. We are indebted to the late Leon Stein, David Von Drehle, Richard Greenwald, Annelise Orleck, Ellen Wiley Todd, Jo Ann Argersinger, and the Kheel Center for their thorough research, through which we found many primary sources, including personal interviews and newspaper accounts. Special thanks to Michael Hirsch for his careful reading of the manuscript.

Unless otherwise noted, all images appear courtesy of Workers United, the successor union to the International Ladies Garment Workers Union (ILGWU) and Union of Needletrades, Industrial, and Textile Employees (UNITE), whose archives are located at the Kheel Center for Labor-Management Documentation and Archives at Cornell University. Other sources of images include the Library of Congress (LC), Brown Brothers (BB), the Schlesinger Library at Radcliffe College (RC), the Yeshiva University Museum (YU), Columbia University Library (CL), the New York City Fire Department Museum (FDNY), the New York Public Library (NYPL), other libraries as noted, and the families of Triangle victims. We thank all for their collaboration in this worthy project.

INTRODUCTION

On Sunday, blazing newspaper headlines told of the Triangle factory fire that had killed more than 100 garment workers the day before—March 25, 1911. It was the largest workplace disaster in New York City history (and remained so until the terrorist attacks of September 11, 2001, on the World Trade Center.) The exact number of workers who died in the Triangle fire was not immediately known. But even in an era when tens of thousands of workers a year perished in industrial accidents, the carnage at Triangle was shocking, especially because the vast majority of the victims were young women—many in their teens—from among the millions of Jewish and Italian immigrants who had come to America to work for a better life.

Now they had died horribly, scores leaping to their deaths in view of helpless and horrified firemen and onlookers to escape the unbearable heat, choking smoke, and searing flames. The fire ladders could only reach the sixth floor, not nearly high enough to save the desperate garment workers trapped on the eighth, ninth, and 10th floors, and the rescue nets broke from the force of falling bodies. The Asch Building at the corner of Washington Place and Greene Street, just a half block from Washington Square Park, *was* fireproof, but the fabric and furnishings burned, and workers in the overcrowded Triangle Waist Company could not get out fast enough to escape the rapidly spreading fire.

Triangle was one of the biggest garment factories in New York, and its owners, Max Blanck and Isaac Harris, were known as the "Shirtwaist Kings." They packed as many sewing machines and operators into the three floors of their factory loft as possible, but the 10,000-square-foot floors of the loft did not have enough exits for a large workforce to quickly exit in case of emergency. The two stairways were so narrow that factory doors, contrary to accepted safety requirements, had to open inward. The two operating elevators were small. The single fire escape was faulty and descended into an airshaft. Sprinklers, although available, were not required by law and never installed, even though the loft was often filled with thousands of pounds of highly flammable material. The Asch Building, 10 years old at the time of the fire, had fulfilled the requirements of the building code of 1900 and regularly passed inspections by the fire and building departments. Fire drills were not mandatory and were never performed. For factory owners insured against financial loss from fire, safety was not a compelling concern. For its part, government was complicit in neglecting workplace safety: the laws were lax and feebly enforced or ignored.

In this period, fires were all too common and factory fires broke out all the time. Triangle was the major disaster waiting to happen. Garment workers and their unions knew the danger and had made their concerns known to employers, government officials, and the public, but to no avail. Labor was weak and safety often took a back seat to pressing demands for higher wages, shorter hours, and union recognition. Even so, the shirtwaist kings adamantly refused to recognize organized labor or acquiesce to any of its demands. Their creation of a company union provoked a strike in 1909 that dragged on without resolution. Local 25 of the International Ladies Garment Workers Union (ILGWU) called a meeting at Cooper Union on November 22nd to consider a course of action. The result was a general strike, known as the "Uprising of the 20,000," a bitter struggle that was waged over the winter of 1909–1910. Although Triangle's owners Blanck and Harris, infamous for antiunion intransigence, made some concessions on wages and hours, they still refused to recognize the union. For garment labor, the disastrous fire that broke out at

Triangle a little more than a year later stood as a ringing condemnation of the shirtwaist kings and other antiunion employers and energized the union cause, especially because some of Triangle's survivors immediately reported that locked factory doors, a common practice to prevent theft, had increased the staggering death toll.

Labor unions responded to the grief and anger of garment workers across the city by organizing a massive funeral procession for seven unidentified victims of the fire; 400,000 turned out on April 5th in a steady rain to walk in or watch the solemn Trade Parade for the Triangle victims. This unprecedented outpouring of sentiment by garment workers and the public signaled their determination to organize and see significant labor reforms enacted. Between 1909 and 1913, union membership in New York City grew from 30,000 to 250,000. Traditionally antiunion Tammany Hall politicians felt the weight of public opinion, which now demanded progressive change. As a result of the work of the Factory Investigating Commission, led by Al Smith, Robert Wagner, and Frances Perkins, more than 30 fire safety laws were quickly passed, saving countless lives and paving the way for the New Deal, an alliance between progressives and trade unionists that established our basic labor rights and ultimately created the mass American middle class.

For the 146 victims and their families and friends, the Triangle Shirtwaist Factory fire was an irredeemable loss. No one could go back and save them, nothing could bring the dead back to life, and no one could replace them in their family or friendship circles. That was and remains a stubborn reality. Even four generations later, and even in families where the memory of this tragedy has become attenuated almost to the brink of being forgotten, slender threads of remembrance can awaken acute feelings of loss, as Sheila Nevins's moving letter to her great-aunt Celia attests.

For the hundreds of thousands of immigrants who were working as sweated garment labor at the time of the Triangle fire, it was the never-to-be-forgotten, never-to-be-repeated holocaust. This tragedy, shocking for its horror and magnitude, was a cataclysm that rent the already frayed fabric of industrial relations and united garment workers in their determination to never let such a disaster happen again. For their descendents, the Triangle fire, although by now a distant memory seldom thought of and imperfectly recalled, nonetheless resonates when brought to mind, because it was such a profoundly shocking event in the life of the founding generation that struggled to secure a place for itself—and us—in a strange but promising land. Immigrants had thought: "In America, they don't let you burn." They learned through tragedy that they would have to wage a monumental struggle to make their chosen land live up to their image of it as a humane place of liberty and justice for all, even for humble immigrant workers.

The strangest thing, perhaps, is that they succeeded in making the United States a much better place than it was. Had the fire not occurred in the context of labor and progressive struggle, there would not have been any historical redemption for the terrible sacrifice of 146 lives, or any remembrance. We do remember, even if imperfectly, to honor their sacrifice and our heritage and to defend our hard won labor rights. Garment manufacturing has largely been exported, and with it the shame of sweatshops and deadly factory fires. We are called by memory of 1911 to finally make *all* workplaces safe.

One

IMMIGRANT LABOR

Jewish and Italian immigrants labored long hours at breakneck speed in harsh and unsafe garment sweatshops. Many recognized that in an inhumane industrial system hard work alone would not suffice to realize their aspirations. As a new century dawned, immigrant workers formed trade unions, organized militant strikes, and gravitated toward socialist politics to fight for, as well as work for, the American dream. Their struggle found organizational form in the International Ladies Garment Workers Union (1900), the Socialist Party of America (1901), the Women's Trade Union League (1903), the Industrial Workers of the World (1905), and the Amalgamated Clothing Workers of America (1914).

In this time of intense labor unrest and radical longings, these and other organizations struggled fiercely to give workers a voice in determining the conditions of their work—a measure of industrial democracy. In fall 1909 a bitter and prolonged strike by women shirtwaist makers at the Triangle and Leiserson companies, two of the biggest firms in the garment industry, erupted into the Uprising of the 20,000, an unprecedented general strike over the winter of 1909–1910 that focused public attention on the plight of garment workers. Although they won some of their demands on wages and hours, Triangle refused to recognize their union. In 1910, a general strike by cloak makers, the "Great Revolt," led to an historic agreement between union and management, the "Protocols of Peace," designed to stabilize the industry by ending labor unrest. But American labor conditions remained brutal, as the Triangle fire of 1911 would dramatically demonstrate. The following year, the Industrial Workers of the World's "Big Bill" Haywood led the long and bitter "Bread and Roses" strike of textile workers in Lawrence, Massachusetts, and Eugene V. Debs, the Socialist Party candidate for U.S. president, garnered nearly one million votes, not nearly enough to win, but more than enough to underline the potential of radical politics in a time of oppressive labor conditions. The Progressive reform agenda that ultimately triumphed was proposed amidst labor protest and radical political challenge.

Through labor unions, strike solidarity, and radical politics, courageous working people confronted the brutal industrial order that dominated their lives. Ultimately, their struggle and sacrifice won the basic labor rights Americans now expect, but only after tens of thousands had perished, including these 146 people. We remember their sacrifice to honor them, to respect our labor heritage, and to defend our hard won rights, which must never be taken for granted.

The Statue of Liberty in New York Harbor welcomed millions of immigrants to the United States. Emma Lazarus's poem, "The New Colossus," is inscribed on its base, with these famous lines: "Give me your tired, your poor, your huddled masses yearning to breathe free, the wretched refuse of your teeming shore. Send these, the homeless, tempest-tost to me, I lift my lamp beside the golden door!" (LC.)

Between 1892 and 1954, Ellis Island processed nearly 12 million immigrants. Historian Oscar Handlin said, "Once I thought to write a history of the immigrants in America. Then I discovered that the immigrants were America." (LC.)

Immigrants on Ellis Island gaze across the harbor at New York City. (LC.)

The busy corner of Orchard and Rivington Streets was in the heart of New York's Lower East Side, densely populated in the early 1900s with Jewish and Italian immigrant families. "The slum is the measure of civilization," wrote Jacob Riis, author of *How the Other Half Lives*. (LC.)

Our Lady of Pompeii served the Italian immigrant population of Greenwich Village at the turn of the 20th century. Many victims of the fire were parishioners and masses were said for them almost daily in the months following the tragedy. A High Requiem Mass for the victims filled the church to overflowing and was marked by the wailing of the many bereaved relatives and friends. (Our Lady of Pompeii.)

Mother Cabrini began her American mission to Italian immigrants in New York City. Here she pioneered the idea of bilingual education and opened a trade school at Our Lady of Pompeii, where immigrant women were taught skills to enter the garment industry. After founding many schools, hospitals, and orphanages in poor communities across the United States, she was canonized as the first American saint. (Cabrini College.)

Opened in 1887 on New York's Lower East Side, the Eldridge Street Synagogue was the "first great East European synagogue [and] expressed the hope that the immigrants' religion and culture would flourish on American soil." (Eldridge Street Synagogue Museum.)

The *Jewish Daily Forward* (*Forverts* in Yiddish) was founded in 1897 by Abraham Cahan and other Jewish socialists as a Yiddish-language daily. As a private publication loosely affiliated with the Socialist Party of America, it achieved massive circulation and considerable political influence during the first three decades of the 20th century.

Tammany Hall, New York City's powerful Democratic Party organization during the Gilded Age, gained electoral support from the city's burgeoning immigrant population, which often exchanged political support for Tammany Hall's patronage, a rudimentary public welfare system. (NYPL.)

"Silent" Charlie Murphy (center, walking) brought respectability to the infamously corrupt Tammany Hall. He promoted a new cohort of politicians that included Al Smith and Robert Wagner, who would reward the loyalty of the poor with reforms like factory safety and child labor laws. This Progressivism drew the votes of the growing number of new immigrants from eastern and southern Europe, which kept Tammany in power until the early 1930s. (LC.)

These four young children were hand sewing garments at home in 1900. Home-work by children brought needed income to poor immigrant families and enriched employers. According to Lewis Hine, journalist and photographer: "There is work that profits children, and there is work that brings profit only to employers. The object of employing children is not to train them, but to get high profits from their work." (LC.)

This c. 1910 photograph by Lewis Hine of an overburdened Italian immigrant woman carrying a bundle of garments on New York's Lower East Side is worth a thousand words about the hard labor immigrants endured to survive.

As the garment industry grew, manufacturers moved out of tenement sweatshops into small factories.

By 1903, most garment manufacturing was done in factories, which employed a division of labor and power-driven machines that drastically increased the pace of work.

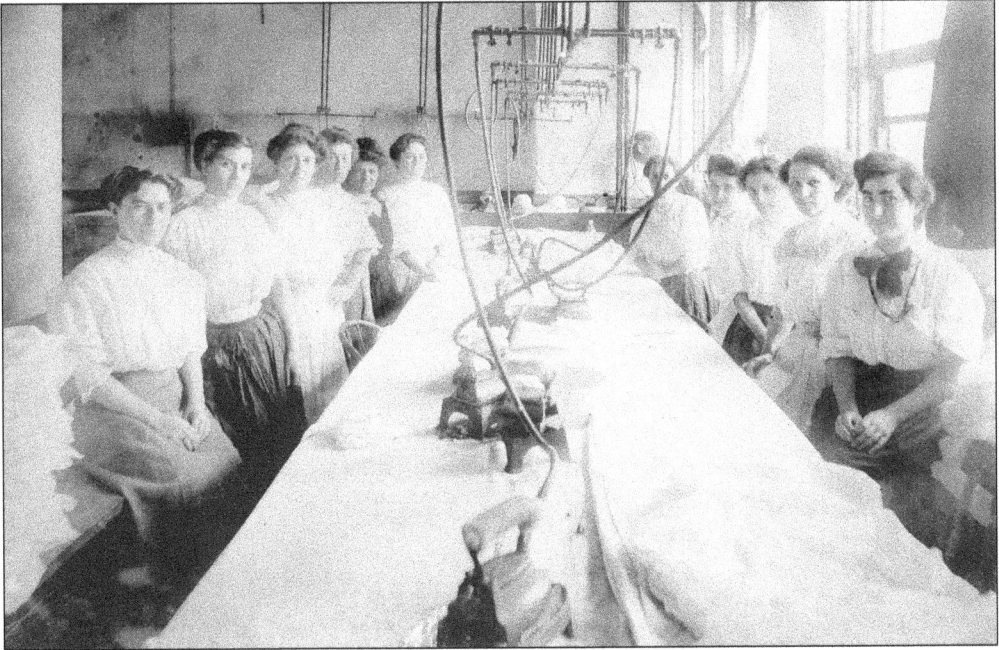

These women pressers were working in an up-to-date factory loft. New York's factory law allowed more workers to be crowded into loft factories because their high ceilings provided the required 250 cubic feet of air. The old sweatshops became work teams gathered under one roof.

The tailors on this large factory floor are working at breakneck speed because all their sewing machines were run by electric power.

Isaac Harris and Max Blanck (first row, center), known as the "Shirtwaist Kings," owned the Triangle Waist Company, which occupied the top three floors of the Asch Building, at the corner of Washington Place and Greene Street. They are seen here amidst their workers and some visitors.

This group portrait shows the women of the Blanck family wearing their fur-trimmed winter finery on an excursion into a wooded area. The attire worn by these women attests to the family's wealth. (Susan Harris.)

The grandeur of this brownstone, Max Blanck's family residence, announced the material success that its immigrant owner earnestly sought and achieved. The Gilded Age was an era of both conspicuous consumption and crushing poverty. (Susan Harris.)

"An Underprice Sensation" is a 1908 advertisement created for R. H. Macy and Company, located on Lower Broadway's "Ladies Mile." The (shirt)waist, a high-necked blouse of crisp, light, translucent cotton or linen, was also featured by illustrator Charles Dana Gibson on his "Gibson Girl" fashion drawings. The New York garment industry supplied retailers with ready-to-wear, washable shirtwaists, jumpers, and skirts, which were worn by women of all social classes. (YU.)

Rose Schneiderman is seen here in 1905, sewing on a machine with a mound of fabric behind her. Born in 1882 in Poland, Rose migrated with her family to the United States in 1890 and by 1898 worked as a lining stitcher in a cap factory on New York's Lower East Side. She organized the first women's local of the United Cloth Hat and Cap Makers Union. Recognized for her role in the 1905 cap makers' strike, she was elected secretary of her local and delegate to the New York Central Labor Union. She soon became active in the Women's Trade Union League (WTUL), which lent moral and financial support to the organizing of women workers. Elected vice president of its New York branch in 1908, she left factory work for a full time position with the WTUL. She played a leading role in the Uprising of the 20,000, worked briefly for the ILGWU, and spent the rest of her long career with the WTUL.

This 1912 group portrait of the ILGWU Local 25 Executive Board includes Clara Lemlich (third row, third from left), Morris Hillquit (second row, second from right), and Benjamin Schlesinger (first row, second from left). Lemlich inspired the 1909 waistmakers' general strike; Hillquit served as legal counsel to the ILGWU and cofounded the Socialist Party, and Schlesinger was an ILGWU president.

The Cooper Union for the
Advancement of Science and Art was
founded by Peter Cooper in 1859. All
its students were awarded full-tuition
scholarships based on merit alone,
regardless of race, religion, sex, or
social status. Located on Astor Place
near the Lower East Side, it hosted
many historic labor, civil rights,
and politically progressive events.

Samuel Gompers, founder and
longtime president of the American
Federation of Labor, promoted
harmony among the different craft
unions of skilled workers and collective
bargaining for shorter hours and higher
wages. He was the featured speaker at a
general strike meeting that was called
by the ILGWU Local 25 and held at
Cooper Union on November 22, 1909.

Samuel Gompers, addressing shirtwaist makers in Cooper Union's Great Hall about a proposed general strike, said that "there comes a time when not to strike is but to rivet the chains of slavery upon our wrists . . . I ask you to stand together, to have faith in yourselves, to be true to your comrades. Let your watchword be Union and progress, and until then no surrender!" The crowd cheered.

People said that Clara Lemlich was *farbrent* (on fire) for the union. She was a fiery speaker who encouraged her sisters to support each other in unionism. After immigrating to the Lower East Side from the Ukraine, Clara began working in garment factories, where miserable working conditions and abusive treatment led her to organize women garment workers into Local 25 of the ILGWU. She courageously endured beatings and arrests on picket lines. Yet she drew strength from sisterhood with women in similar situations and from the WTUL, which supported the shirtwaist strikers and worked towards women's suffrage.

Even after Samuel Gompers roused the crowd at Cooper Union with fiery rhetoric, no vote was called. Clara Lemlich, a committed socialist and founding member of Local 25, made her way to the stage, shouting in Yiddish, "I want to say a few words!" At the podium, she continued, "I have listened to all the speakers, and I have no further patience for talk. I am a working girl, one of those striking against intolerable conditions. I am tired of listening to speakers who talk in generalities. What we are here for is to decide whether or not to strike. I offer a resolution that a general strike be declared." The audience rose and cheered and took a traditional Yiddish oath—"If I turn traitor to the cause I now pledge, may this hand wither from the arm I now raise." Their general strike became known as the Uprising of the 20,000.

Because a labor strike can succeed only by preventing the company from operating, unions set up picket lines to keep strikebreakers from being employed. In this photograph, waistmakers enthusiastically volunteer to picket, despite the threat of beatings and arrests.

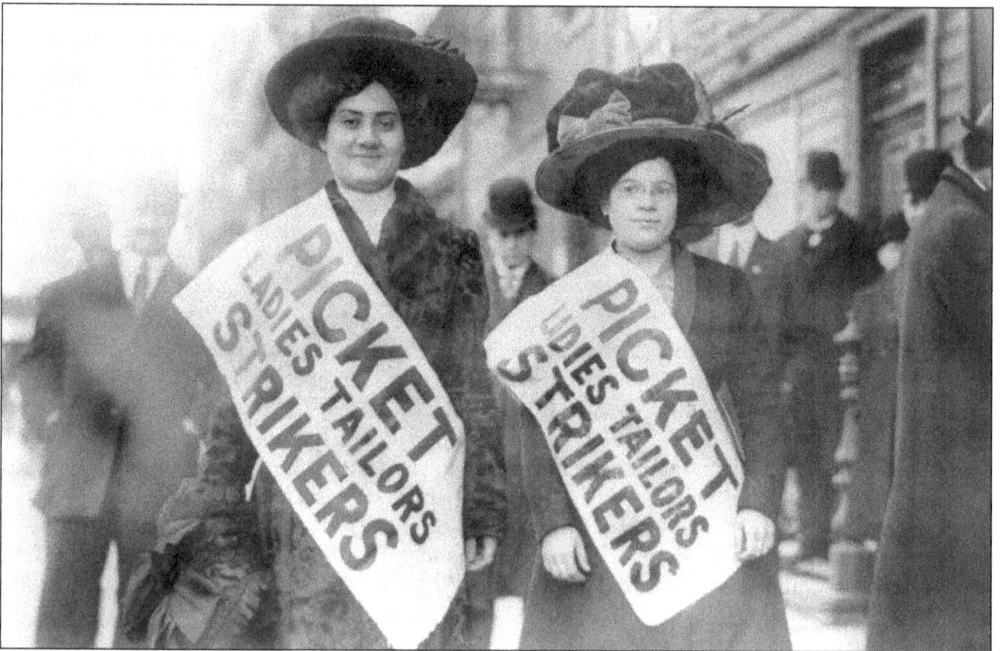

These two picketers are dressed in their best clothing and proudly display sashes declaring that they are striking ladies tailors who are doing picket duty. Picket lines, in addition to discouraging strikebreakers, also serve to inform the public, whose sympathy and support are needed for victory.

Striking waistmakers in the Uprising of the 20,000 of 1909–1910 were routinely beaten and arrested. Here a police wagon or "Black Mariah" has brought arrested strikers to Night Court at the Jefferson Market Courthouse, where they were tried alongside prostitutes, a humiliation meant to discourage them from picketing.

During the shirtwaist makers strike of 1909–1910, women arrested on the picket line were tried in the Jefferson Market Courthouse, a landmark Victorian Gothic structure built in 1877. (LC.)

This 1909 newspaper photograph is captioned, "Girls who served on Blackwell's Island and were cheered last night." These women had been arrested and sent to the prison workhouse as a result of their strike activities. The demure-looking women in this "rogue's gallery" obviously wear their signs as badges of honor to shame authorities, arouse public sympathy, and embolden fellow strikers. They were cheered upon release. (Blackwell's Island is now Roosevelt Island.)

Hundreds of shirtwaist strikers met at Carnegie Hall wearing sashes marked "arrested." This meeting, organized by wealthy WTUL strike supporters, was designed to engender public sympathy.

The Women's Trade Union League was founded in 1903. It served a major supporting role in the Uprising of the 20,000 and was influential in expanding membership in the ILGWU. Wealthy WTUL supporters like Alva Belmont, Anne Morgan, Mary Dreier, and college women fought alongside working-class women like Rose Schneiderman, Leonora O'Reilly, Pauline Newman, and Clara Lemlich to promote unionization and women's suffrage.

The ladies of the Women's Trade Union League of New York display their organization banner, proclaiming "The 8 Hour Day."

This photograph, taken December 3, 1909, shows six women, including leaders of the Women's Trade Union League, linked arm in arm in their march to city hall. The WTUL in New York was led by affluent reformers and suffragettes, who saw themselves as "allies" of working-class women.

Carola Woerishoffer, a young, wealthy graduate of Bryn Mawr, used her resources to buy houses, and then, waiting in the Jefferson Market Court, offered their deeds as security for strikers' release.

Inez Milholland, a New York City lawyer, was a member of the WTUL and supporter of women's suffrage. In this 1909 photograph, she drove her own car in a march of shirtwaist strikers. (BB.)

The headquarters of the WTUL was busy during the uprising. Rose Schneiderman (center, looking left) and Leonora O'Reilly (at the telephone) are among the WTUL members shown in this photograph.

Close working relationships engendered strong feelings. This photograph of Clara Lemlich and Pauline Newman was taken in 1910, shortly after the conclusion of the Uprising of the 20,000. Pauline Newman worked at the Triangle Waist Company for over seven years and became close friends with her coworkers and with union sisters like Clara Lemlich. Newman shared a letter she received from a coworker, who wrote, "We shall be friends in joy and sorrow! What is there sweeter in life than the sympathy between woman and woman—what purer than the sincerity of hearts—what greater than the harmony of minds?" (RC.)

This photograph, which appeared in *Munsey's Magazine* in 1910, shows women shirtwaist strikers selling donated copies of the *New York Call*, New York's socialist daily. A placard with Hebrew writing hangs in the background. Clearly, during the Progressive Era there was an intimate relationship between labor unionism and socialist politics on New York's Lower East Side, especially among Jewish workers.

Striking garment workers march on city hall carrying a sign that calls for a union contract.

The large number of striking garment workers seen here illustrates the magnitude of the general strike. The presence of so many strikers made the strike a significant public event.

Mass demonstrations organized by the ILGWU were a powerful display of the union's newfound strength and determination.

Italian and Jewish cloak makers carry picket signs written in Italian and in Yiddish. They created different union locals in order to run meetings in the languages of the members. Nonetheless, in the course of labor struggle, they achieved solidarity across ethnic and religious lines.

Striking trade unionists holding placards march through New York City streets in 1910.

These striking cloak makers, dressed in their best clothing and riding in a horse-drawn carriage, display their union loyalty. Their sign reads, "Long Live the Cloak Makers Union. Employees of Jouvenile Cloak Co. 327 E 29 St."

These humble Jewish immigrants are requesting donations for striking cloak makers. The sign on their cart reads: "We are collecting Provisions for Striking Tailors. Please help." The union had little in the way of strike funds, and garment workers had little or no personal financial reserves. Severe deprivation could force surrender.

Meyer London, a leader of the "Great Revolt" of cloak makers in 1910, proclaimed, "This general strike is greater than any union. It is an irresistible movement of the people. It is a protest against conditions that can no longer be tolerated . . . some of the men working sixteen hours a day during the hottest month of the year while thousands of others have no employment whatever."

Louis D. Brandeis, son of European Jewish immigrants, was dubbed the "peoples lawyer." He fought against powerful corporations, monopolies, and public corruption, and framed the "Protocol of Peace," a landmark industry-wide agreement between the ILGWU and garment manufacturers that set standards for wages, hours, and job conditions. It established a bureaucracy of labor, management, and the "public" to mediate inevitable disputes. He served as a U.S. Supreme Court justice (1916–1939).

The embrace between management and labor, which represents the "Protocol of Peace," is fraught by their potential use of deadly weapons against one another; the bosses threaten lockout and the workers a strike. The original title and caption of this illustration by Lola read, "Peace Talk at the Point of a Dagger"; "He: 'Do you love me kitten . . . ?' She: 'Certainly just as much as you love me.'"

Two

FIRE!

At closing time on Saturday, March 25, 1911, a fire broke out on the eighth floor of the Triangle Waist Company. Despite efforts to contain it with buckets of water, the fire rapidly spread through the overcrowded factory, as did panic among workers rushing toward the loft's few exits, which were quickly obstructed by fire or people desperately trying to escape by elevator, narrow stairway, or faulty fire escape. Warned by phone, those on the 10th floor escaped to the roof. But no one warned sewing machine operators on the ninth floor. When the fire reached them, a locked door, or exit doors blocked by the crush of panicked workers, prevented their escape from the suffocating smoke, unbearable heat, and searing flames. Despite the multiple trips made by heroic elevator operators, many frantic workers were left behind.

Surrounded by flames, scores ran to the windows, from which they leapt to their deaths while firemen and citizens looked on helpless and horrified. The fire ladders could only reach to the sixth floor and the rescue nets did not hold against the force of bodies falling from such a great height, some of which broke through the deadlights in the sidewalk to the basement below. Water from fire hoses would soon extinguish the flames, but it was too late for 146 Triangle workers. The sight of so many people plummeting to their deaths profoundly shook consumer activist Frances Perkins, who reached the scene just as workers began to jump. Even veteran firefighters were overcome by the magnitude of the horror. The belongings gathered up by the police from the sidewalks were taken to the Mercer Street Police Station. The bodies were taken to the Charities Pier on East Twenty-sixth Street to be identified by relatives.

For many survivors, desperate struggle to escape immediately gave way to frantic fear for a sister or friend whose fate was still unknown. As news of the fire rapidly spread by word of mouth, waves of fear for relatives and friends swept over working-class neighborhoods. From the Lower East, thousands came running to the Asch Building. Soon dread was followed by the joy of finding a loved one alive or, all too often, the agony of identifying a mangled body in the temporary morgue. Every grief stricken family was devastated. For the whole garment labor force, the enormity of the loss was staggering. By the following day, the disaster was headline news across a horrified city and country.

The Bain Collection of the Library of Congress identifies this photograph as "Horse-drawn fire engines in street, on their way to the Triangle Shirtwaist Company fire, New York City." Fireman Frank Rubino recalled, "We came tearing down Washington Square East and made the turn into Washington Place. The first thing I saw was a man's body come crashing through the sidewalk shed of the school building. We kept going." (LC.)

Firemen used newly invented high-pressure hoses to fight the Triangle fire. The Asch Building was in one of the first areas with high water pressure. Fireman Frank Rubino recounted, "As we turned on to Greene Street and began to stretch our hoses, the bodies were hitting all around us." (BB.)

The *New York Times* reported, "From high water towers and from ten hose lines firemen continued to pour steady streams into the top floors of the building. The water smacked the face of the building with a loud sound . . . it came cascading out of the windows, down the sides, out of the lobby, falling like a miniature Niagara, and turning the gutter into a blood-stained rivulet."

Police and bystanders gaze at the upper floors of the Asch Building as bodies lie on the street at their feet. Company 20 had the tallest ladder in the fire department, but it could only reach to the sixth floor. Chief Edward J. Worth stated, "The men did the best they could. But there is no apparatus in the department to cope with this kind of fire."

The impact of falling bodies broke through the "cellar deadlights" of glass embedded in the sidewalk to provide daylight to the underground vault below the Asch Building. Chief Edward J. Worth reported: "What good were life nets? The little ones went through life net, pavement, and all . . . I didn't know that they would come down . . . three and even four together." (BB.)

Police place colored and numbered tags on each body. Reporter William Gunn Shepherd stated, "I remembered their great strike last year in which these same girls had demanded more sanitary conditions and more safety precautions in the shops. These dead bodies were the answer."

Police lean over the dead. Bodies were laid out and tagged. According to *New York World*, "At intervals throughout the night, the very horror of their task overcame the most experienced policeman and morgue attaches. The crews were completely changed no less than three times."

During the night, police and firemen brought out bodies to place them into coffins. The *New York Sun* reported: "Worming their way through the clutter of ambulances, mounted policemen, patrol wagons and throbbing fire engines, came men bearing rough hewn coffins on their shoulders. The police had sent for 75 to 100 coffins. But all they had was 65." (LC.)

Police carry baskets of items scattered along the street. According to the *New York Sun*, policemen "began to glean the cheap belongings the girls had clutched as they fell through space. There were leather handbags, broken combs, hair ribbons, some dimes and cents, parts of clothing. In the gutter water, policeman picked up what appeared to be a necklace but which under the electric light proved to be a rosary."

Firemen lower tarpaulin-wrapped bodies from the ninth floor. The *New York World* reported: "As each body was started down, the bright beam of a searchlight picked out its dark outline and followed it to the street . . . On the sidewalk a squad of policemen reached up as each body came to the end of its spotlighted journey." (BB.)

This photograph shows a fireman stationed at a window in the burned factory, to assist in lowering the bodies by swinging each clear of the windowsill as it passed.

This is a view of the burned ninth floor with sewing machines visible on the tables. According to the *New York World*, Chief Edward Croker saw sights "that utterly staggered him, that sent him, a man used to viewing horrors, back down into the street with quivering lips."

This is a view of the airshaft of the Asch Building, where the fire escape led down to a skylight on the second floor. The windows that led to the fire escape were covered by iron shutters, held closed by metal pins, which opened outward on to the fire escape. (BB.)

The intense heat of the fire melted and twisted the fire escape. Survivor Nellie Ventura remembered, "At first I was too frightened to try to run through the fire. Then I heard the screams of the girls inside. I knew I had to go down the ladder or die where I was."

This is a newspaper photograph of the narrow, windowless staircase on the Washington Place side of the Asch Building that ended at the 10th floor, with no exit to the roof. At 2 feet, 9 inches wide, the stairway was so narrow that factory doors, contrary to safety guidelines, could only open inward.

This photograph provides a closer view of the fire escape and iron shutters that were twisted by the intense heat of the fire. "I still had one foot on the fire escape when I heard a loud noise and looked back up. The people were falling all around me, screaming all around me. The fire escape was collapsing," recounted survivor Abe Gordon. (BB.)

"The Worthless Fire Escape and the Death Trap Below It" offered newspaper readers a detailed and labeled view of the "broken fire escape that led many to death" and the "fatal pit beneath from which twenty-five bodies were taken." Some victims crashed through the skylight to the cellar below and others were impaled on the iron picket fence at the bottom of the airshaft.

LETTING DOWN A VICTIM'S BODY.
Note the expensive and elaborate ornamentation around the windows in terrible contrast with the awful result of the lack of fire-fighting and life-saving facilities.

THE BUILDING AT THE HEIGHT OF THE FIRE.
The structure itself, which is situated at Greene Street and Washington Place, was fireproof, but the contents could hardly have been more inflammable. Note Washington Square a block north of the building.

THE ONE INADEQUATE FIRE ESCAPE.
Looking down the shaft. Although warped and twisted, there is enough left to show how impossible it was for this one escape to serve 600 or more persons.

VIEW OF INTERIOR AFTER THE DISASTER.
For the floor area of the building there should have been three instead of two stairways; on the other hand, the moral of the fire is that an insufficient law is much to blame.

WHERE THE FIRE STARTED.
The tub shown figured in several ineffectual attempts to put out the fire. Standpipes and hose at hand were not used. A fire drill might have saved all.

TOP OF ELEVATOR.
Panic-stricken girls plunged down the shaft crashing in with their bodies the top of the elevator.

SCENE AT THE TEMPORARY MORGUE.
The number of victims was so great that the Department of Charities pier was pressed into service to receive the bodies. Not since the Slocum disaster has New York had such an experience.

THE DOORS THAT OPENED INWARD.
Whether or not the doors were locked, it is declared they opened inward, in itself a very dangerous condition.

SHUTTERS OBSTRUCTING ESCAPES.
The fire escape had treads eighteen inches in width, and was so constructed that when iron shutters on windows were opened it was impossible for persons to use them without first closing the shutters.

THE LIVING VICTIMS.
One of hundreds of the grief-stricken friends who came to identify the bodies of the dead.

WHERE THE BODIES FELL.
The unfortunate girls plunging from the upper stories broke the iron and glass work on the sidewalk with the force of their fall.

This collection of Triangle fire photographs shows where the fire started on the eighth floor (second row from top, right), the elevator roof caved in from falling bodies (third row, left), a door that opened inward (third row, right), a distraught family leaving the morgue (bottom row, center), and officials viewing the hole in the sidewalk deadlights made by a falling body (bottom row, right). (NYPL.)

52

Two heroic elevator operators, Joseph Zito and Gaspar Mortillalo, probably rescued 150 people, about half the survivors. Zito recalled, "When I first opened the elevator door on the ninth floor all I could see was a crowd of girls and men with great flames and smoke right behind them. When I came to the floor the [last] time, the girls were standing on the window sills with the fire all around them."

Crowds soon gathered at the Asch Building. The *New York Tribune* reported, "In the center of this square of sorrowing humanity, rising like a giant tombstone, the blackened and scarred building reared skyward."

It was estimated that by 5:00 p.m., about 10,000 people had arrived at the scene of the fire. According to the *New York World*: "Great hordes came marching up from the East Side." The crowds returned the following day.

SCENE OF WASHINGTON PLACE FIRE

The morning following the fire, the streets around the Asch Building were eerily empty as crowds were held back by police lines at Waverly Place on the north, Mercer Street on the east, West Fourth Street on the south, and the edge of Washington Square on the west.

CROWDS AT SENCE OF WASHINGTON ST. FIRE N.Y. 3/26/11.

A crowd gathered in Washington Square Park one block away from the Triangle factory building. This gathering was an incongruous mix of both the grief stricken and idle curiosity seekers. (LC.)

FIREMEN SEARCHING FOR BODIES 3/26/11

The caption of this photograph from the Bain Collection of the Library of Congress states: "Firemen searching for bodies 3/26/11." Leon Stein notes that on Sunday morning firemen discovered two bodies in the basement, hanging over the steam pipes behind the boiler. The emotional toll of this work is evident in the bearing of the fireman leaning against a building abutment. (LC.)

56

The city's morgue was too small to hold all the dead, so a temporary morgue was set up on a covered East River pier at the foot of East Twenty-sixth Street. "The Charities Pier" had also been used as a morgue after the 1904 *General Slocum* steamboat fire tragedy, when the street was nicknamed "Misery Lane." This photograph shows the great number of people lining up to enter the morgue.

OUTSIDE PIER MORGUE 3|26|11

A policeman stands guard and keeps order outside the pier morgue, where the bereaved and the curious lined up to view the Triangle victims. (LC.)

The *New York World* reported: "The cavernous pier is the stage of all the abject tragedies of the city." (BB.)

In this retouched photograph, families walk along the row of coffins to identify their missing loved ones.

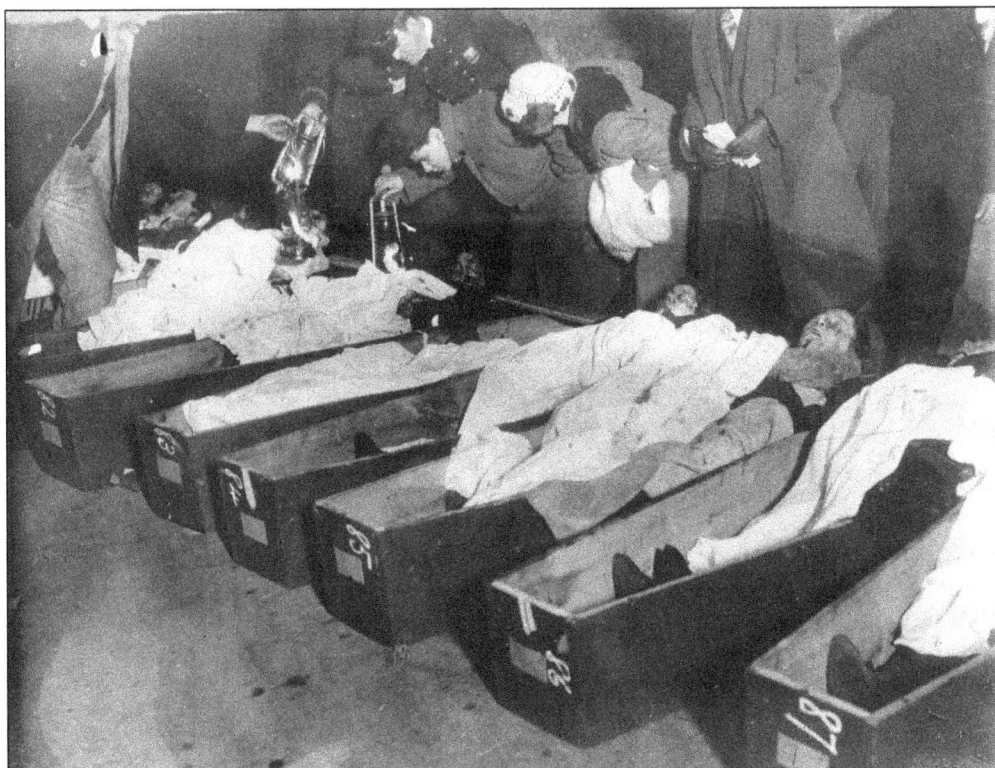

At the morgue, the bodies lay in long rows of numbered coffins, covered by white sheets, with their heads propped up on boards for easier recognition by loved ones. Police with lanterns facilitated identification. According to Leon Stein: "The experienced morgue attendants had arranged the bodies so that those in the worst condition were farthest from the doors. In this way it was thought the hardships for friends and family would be minimized." (BB.)

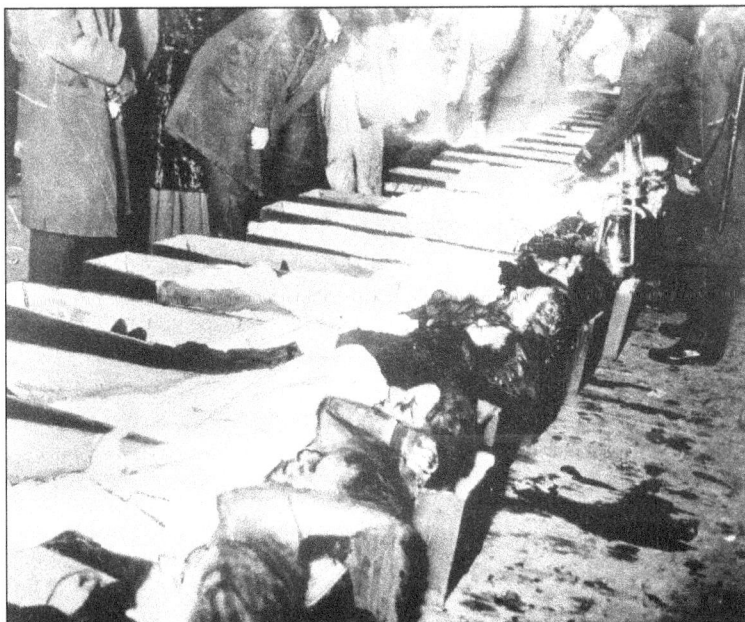

According to the *New York World*, at the pier morgue, when "bodies were so utterly incinerated as to make recognition impossible by other than bits of jewelry, the finger rings, necklaces and earrings were not removed. Policemen were especially assigned to guard these coffins."

Newspapers published lists of the dead as they were identified. Cartoons such as this one, sarcastically captioned "THE PRODUCT OF A "SAFE" FACTORY" and published in the *New York Evening Journal,* Monday, March 27, 1911, began to appear on editorial pages. It depicts the identification of victims at the temporary morgue.

NEW-YORK, MONDAY, MARCH 27, 1911.—TWELVE PAGES.

THE PRODUCT OF A "SAFE" FACTORY

IN COMPLIANCE WITH LAW?
The fire escape that ends in midair must be abolished.

"In Compliance With Law? The fire escape that ends in midair must be abolished." A cartoon by Boardman Robinson in the *New York Tribune* shows women falling off the fire escape and being impaled on the metal picket fence in the airshaft.

This front page of the *New York Evening Journal* of March 28, 1911, reports on the "barred doors" and asks who is responsible. The hangman's noose (bottom right) awaits the guilty.

This Is One of a Hundred Murdered

Is any one to be punished for this?

"This Is One of a Hundred Murdered. Is any one to be punished for this?" This cartoon by Tad appeared in the *New York Evening Journal, Il Progresso,* and in many other newspapers. It shows a dead female dressed in a shirtwaist and skirt on the sidewalk outside a building that has a sign on its door: "Operators Wanted. Inquire Ninth Floor."

This editorial cartoon shows a skeleton wearing the uniform and badge of a building inspector, next to a sign posted on the building, which reads, "RECORD FIRE FOR NEW YORK. 145 LIVES LOST!!!! BUILDING FIRE PROOF. ONLY FIRE ESCAPE COLLAPSES." The signature says: "O.K. INSPECTOR."

In this wordless editorial cartoon, a skeleton rises from the flames of the Asch Building. The artist drew the figures of people jumping from both sides of the building.

This editorial cartoon appeared first in the *New York Evening Journal*, March 31, 1911. The shut door, behind which desperate workers trying to escape the all-consuming flames are trapped, is being held closed by greed, a bald figure covered in money, clothed in dollar bills. He represents the factory owner whose hunger for profits outweighs his regard for the lives of his employees.

Sloan in New York Call.

"HERE IS THE REAL TRIANGLE."

This cartoon by John Sloan appeared in the *New York Call*. Sloan, art editor of *The Masses*, rushed to the nearby Asch Building. That evening he wrote in his diary: "Over one hundred and forty shirtwaist workers were burned to death in the Triangle Factory. These girls made the successful strike of the last year!"

Even though the 10th floor burned, all but one person survived. Warned of the fire by telephone from the eighth floor, Blanck and Harris, as well as employees and visitors, were able to escape to the roof, where New York University law students assisted them.

Three

MOURNING AND PROTEST

As the horrific dimensions of the Triangle fire tragedy quickly became apparent, private grief and anger became palpable communal emotions that alternated, entwined, and found collective expression. All garment workers and their families knew that they were at risk because of greedy bosses, incompetent or corrupt government officials, and a public indifferent to their plight. Anguish over these clearly preventable deaths inexorably led to rage and assignment of blame. Some even sought to kill Blanck and Harris. Although others called for respectful expressions of grief, public mourning predictably merged with mass protest for reforms.

The fire had followed a long and hard fought general strike over oppressive conditions in garment manufacturing. Triangle had intransigently opposed unionization. The government, which had notoriously perpetrated the merciless beatings and mass arrests of strikers, had not—it was now shamefully clear—enacted or enforced building codes to protect their lives. The dead bodies on the street, union leaders and progressives declared, were a resounding indictment of prevailing employer-oriented politics. Had government not sided with employers in their opposition to organized labor, the tragedy at Triangle might have been prevented. Because the fire broke out in the midst of labor and progressive agitation, it became a pivotal moment in the struggle for unionization and labor reform.

On April 5, four-hundred thousand turned out in a steady downpour to walk in or witness a solemn procession for seven unidentified victims. Sixty unions organized this parade to simultaneously express grief and outrage. Amidst the cries of onlookers, they marched silently wearing badges that read, "WE MOURN OUR LOSS." The hitherto antiunion leaders of New York City's Democratic Party machine, Tammany Hall, were persuaded by this massive outpouring of grief to finally embrace reform. Through the work of the Factory Investigating Commission, over 30 fire safety laws were passed, putting New York on a progressive path toward the New Deal. Union militancy continued. The membership rolls of the ILGWU swelled, paving the way for it to become one of the most powerful and politically influential unions in the country. The Triangle owners, Blanck and Harris, were tried for manslaughter—charged with illegally locking a factory door—but were acquitted with the help of a brilliant attorney and a sympathetic judge. Their acquittal, which angered bereaved relatives and garment workers who continued to believe them guilty, unquestionably energized movements for labor reforms now considered essential.

Lantern slides were early colorized and subtitled slide shows, created for group exhibition. (The accuracy of the captions, not reproduced here, cannot always be determined.) These lantern slides are from the collection of Juanita Hadwin, donated to the Kheel Center. In this slide, the grief of this family leaving the pier morgue can be read on their faces. The older woman holds a handkerchief to wipe away the tears.

A grief-stricken family sits outside the morgue.

Women leaving the morgue are holding handkerchiefs to their tearful faces. A uniformed policeman remains by the door.

For any survivor who lost someone in the fire, surviving meant enduring unbearable loss. For those who lost more than one relative or friend in the fire, the grief was overwhelming.

This family outside the morgue is grieving for a lost loved one. (BB.)

Tragically this scene of a family trailing behind the body of a Triangle fire victim they have identified was repeated over and over again. Each family, often with help from organizations such as the Joint Relief Committee, Hebrew Burial Society, or Red Cross, had to bury its dead and cope with their own deep sense of loss.

This slide shows the funeral of Yetta Rosenbaum. Families were large and had many neighbors and friends in the crowded working-class neighborhoods of New York. The funeral of a Triangle fire victim was also a matter of public sympathy and interest.

A grieving family walks behind a hearse that carries a Triangle fire victim.

This scene is described in a lantern slide as the interior of a Catholic church in the Italian district. A family held vigil over two matching white coffins for Triangle fire victims.

THE POPULAR FIRE SONG

DIE FIRE KORBUNES
דיא פייער קרבנות

MUSIC BY
D. MEYROWITZ

WORDS BY
LOUIS GILROD

ARRANGED BY
JACK KAMMEN

VIOLIN 30

THEODORE LOHR
280 GRAND ST. N.Y.

PIANO 50

The popular fire song "Die Fire Korbunes" ("Victims of Fire") was written in 1911. This lament has been translated from Yiddish by Yelena Shmulenson and Allen Rickman of Metropolitan Klezmer. *Korbunes* in Yiddish suggests burnt offerings. The song includes the refrain: "Mothers cry, fathers curse, Say *kaddish* [Jewish prayers for the dead] for young children/ Pain, hurt; it's a disgrace—Sacrifices to the Land of the Dollar." (LC.)

Kalman Donick is pictured here with his wife, Sarah, who was devastated by the loss of her husband. Their baby daughter was 11 months old when Kalman died in the Triangle fire. (Steinberg family.)

Kalman Donick's gravestone at the Hebrew Free Burial Association's cemetery at Mount Richmond in Staten Island, New York, reads: "MY BELOVED FATHER/ KALMAN DONICK/ DIED MARCH 25, 1911/ AGE 26 YEARS." (Rob Linné.)

The Joint Relief Committee report on Rose Oringer states: "R. O., 19 years old, earned $10.00 a week, union member, killed. Father tailor, earns $8.00 to $10.00 a week; mother G., rheumatic, accustomed to go to Sharon Springs every spring for rheumatism; G., 20 years old, driver at Macy's; I., 17 years old, three under school ages, another brother, P., an actor, does not live home. Jewish Burial Society, Adas Israel, buried R. $280.00 relief given family. Total, $280.00." (Philip Maier.)

This photograph shows Rose's family around 1930; pictured are her nephew David (first row, seated left), who became a federal judge for the Occupational Safety and Health Administration; her sister, Ida (second row, second from left); her mother, Gussie (second row, third from left); her father, Louis (second row, fourth from left); her oldest brother Philip (third row, left); her brother George (third row, fifth from left); and other family members. (Philip Maier.)

Rose Oringer's death certificate reads: "(19), Cutter, DC #10112, 65 East 101st Street." Rose was born in 1892 in an eastern province of the Austro-Hungarian Empire, in a village near Chernivtsi in the Bukovina (now in Ukraine), and had lived in the United States for 10 years. She died of her injuries at St Vincent's Hospital on March 25, 1911. The cause of death was: "Fracture of left femur, thigh, & tibia, internal hemorrhaging, jumped from window." Rose was buried at Mount Zion Cemetery in Queens on March 27, 1911. The map below created for the Chalk Project shows where Triangle victims lived. (Right, Michael Hirsch; below, Ruth Sergel.)

Forty-four Triangle fire victims are buried at Mount Zion Cemetery in Queens. Monuments that memorialize the Triangle fire victims include one by the ILGWU and an obelisk dedicated by the Workmen's Circle that reads: "Triangle Shirtwaist Factory Fire. March 25, 1911. WE REMEMBER THE VICTIMS OF THIS TRAGIC EVENT AND STRIVE TO ACHIEVE SAFE WORKING CONDITIONS AND DIGNITY FOR ALL IN A *SHENERE UN A BESERE VELT*—A MORE BEAUTIFUL AND BETTER WORLD." (Michael Hirsch.)

The Triangle Fire Memorial to the Unknowns by Evelyn Longman was erected in the Evergreens Cemetery in Brooklyn in 1912. It was not announced via any unveiling ceremony or publicity and was not embraced by the community or the ILGWU until years later.

"How soon will they be all forgotten?" is the title of this contemporaneous editorial cartoon. This question is still compelling 100 years after the fire.

How Soon Will They Be All Forgotten?

Protests began right after the fire. Here mourners' picket signs are hung with black crepe. Their signs connect nonunion shops to fire traps.

Rose Schneiderman addressed a memorial meeting in the old Metropolitan Opera House (rented by Anne Morgan) on April 2, 1911; garment workers sat in the balconies and wealthy WTUL supporters occupied the orchestra seats. She delivered a brief, powerful indictment of the city's economic and political elite: "I would be a traitor to these poor burned bodies if I came here to talk good fellowship. We have tried you good people of the public and we have found you wanting. The old Inquisition had its rack and its thumbscrews and its instruments of torture with iron teeth. We know what these things are today; the iron teeth are our necessities, the thumbscrews are the high-powered and swift machinery close to which we must work, and the rack is here in the firetrap structures that will destroy us the minute they catch on fire . . . This is not the first time girls have been burned alive in the city . . . The life of men and women is so cheap and property is so sacred."

Rose Schneiderman continued, "We have tried you citizens; we are trying you now, and you have a couple of dollars for the sorrowing mothers, brothers and sisters by way of a charity gift. But every time the workers come out in the only way they know to protest against conditions which are unbearable the strong hand of the law is allowed to press down heavily upon us. Public officials have only words of warning to us—warning that we must be intensely peaceable, and they have the workhouse just back of all their warnings. The strong hand of the law beats us back, when we rise, into the conditions that make life unbearable. I can't talk fellowship to you who are gathered here. Too much blood has been spilled. I know from my experience it is up to the working people to save themselves. The only way they can save themselves is by a strong working-class movement."

Fellow Workers!

Join in rendering a last sad tributè of sympathy and affection for the victims of the Triangle Fire. THE FUNERAL PROCESSION will take place Wednesday, April 5th, at 1 P. M. Watch the newspapers for the line of march.

צו דער לויה שוועסטער אן ברידער!

די לויה פון די היילינע קרבנות פון דעם טרייענגעל פייר וועם זיין סימוואך, דעם 5טען אפריל, 1 אזהר נאכמיטטאג.

קיינער פון אייך מעד נים פערבלייבען אין די שעפער! שליסם זיך צו אין די רייהען פון די מארטשירענדע! דריקם אוים אייער סימפאטיע און מיטגעפיל בעדיירערן אייף דעם נרויסען פערלוסם וואם די ארבייטערוועלט האם געהאם.

נעבייינעז די קעס — סים צימעתתע הערצער זעלעז סיר פיהרען אונזערע מהיייתע שוועסטרע צו זיירער לעצטער רוה.

וואפסטם די צייסוונגען דורך וועלכע סיר וועלען לאזען וויסען וואו איהר קענט זיך צואמטנוקוסען.

צו דער לויה פון די היילינע קרבנות, קומט שוועסטער אן ברידער!

Operai Italiani!

Unitevi compatti a rendere l'ultimo tributo d'affetto alle vittime dell'imane sciagura della Triangle Waist Co. IL CORTEO FUNEBRE avrà luogo mercoledì, 5 Aprile, alle ore 1 P. M. Traverete nei giornali l'ordine della marcia.

This handbill, written in English, Yiddish, and Italian, says, "Fellow Workers! Join in rendering a last sad tribute of sympathy and affection for the victims of the Triangle Fire. THE FUNERAL PROCESSION will take place on April 5th at 1 P. M. Watch the newspapers for the line of march." Fr. Antonio Demo of Our Lady of Pompeii, as well as rabbis and ministers around New York City, allowed the WTUL and the unions to distribute these flyers.

Fr. Antonio Demo of Our Lady of Pompeii actively advocated for his immigrant parishioners through immigration assistance and work skills training. He ministered to the victims' families and allowed organizers to distribute leaflets to parishioners calling for workplace reform. In 1935, thousands attended funeral services for the beloved pastor, and soon after a public plaza in Greenwich Village was dedicated as "Father Demo Square." (Our Lady of Pompeii.)

The *New York Call* (April 5, 1911) announced the union-sponsored procession with the headline: "300,000 WILL DROP THEIR WORK TODAY TO HONOR 143 VICTIMS," and reported that the city's Commissioner of Charities had decided to have the remains of the unidentified victims buried in a municipal plot in the privately owned Evergreens Cemetery. The image of a crucified worker was intended to inflame passions.

On April 5, 1911, four-hundred thousand people walked in or watched the Trade Parade, organized by 60 trade unions, for seven unidentified victims of the Triangle fire. Horses draped with black netting pulled an empty hearse decked with flowers. Marchers walked silently in a steady downpour.

Thousands of mourners surround a horse-drawn, flower-strewn but empty hearse, which symbolically carried the unidentified Triangle fire victims.

Mourners from the Ladies Waist and Dressmakers Union Local 25 and the United Hebrew Trades of New York marched in the streets. Their large banners read: "We mourn our loss." Their silent, dignified proclamation of mass grief clearly also conveyed a message of protest.

Mourners who gathered alongside the funeral procession route to honor the Triangle fire victims in a steady downpour carried umbrellas, which are seen here massed on both sides of the street.

The Trade Parade for the seven unidentified Triangle victims proceeded silently through Washington Square Park in a steady rain, within sight of the Asch Building.

This *New York Tribune* photograph shows workers carrying a union banner in the Trade Parade for unidentified Triangle victims. A large number of onlookers lined the route that passed through Washington Square. The caption read: "A SILENT PARADE OF 50,000." The garment workers and many others in New York marched in silence for many hours in a pouring rain in memory of those who lost their lives in the Triangle factory fire.

Unionists who walked in the Trade Parade for Triangle victims wore mourning badges. This one from Cloak Tailors Union Local 9 proclaims "WE MOURN OUR LOSS, April 5, 1911."

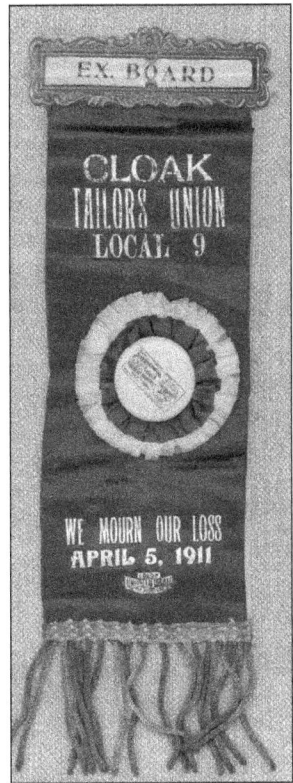

Just five days after the Triangle fire, the owners reopened the Triangle Waist Company on University Place. They bought newspaper advertisements to inform vendors and customers. The publisher of the *New York Call,* out of deference to the fire victims, rejected this check for $250 for a half-page advertisement in the Sunday edition.

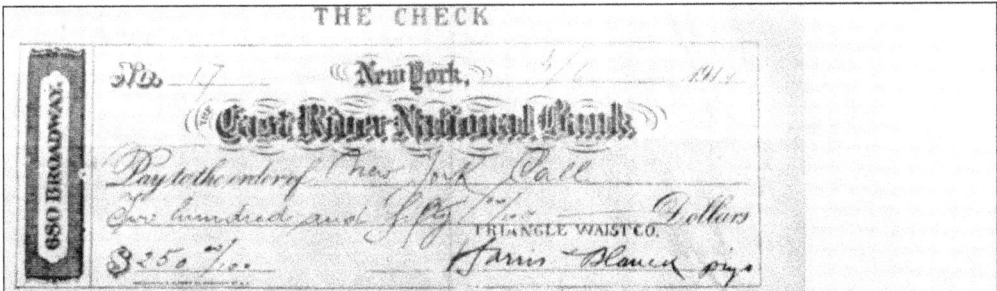

THE CHECK

Offered by Harris & Blanck, proprietors of the Triangle Waist Company, for a half-page advertisement in The Call.

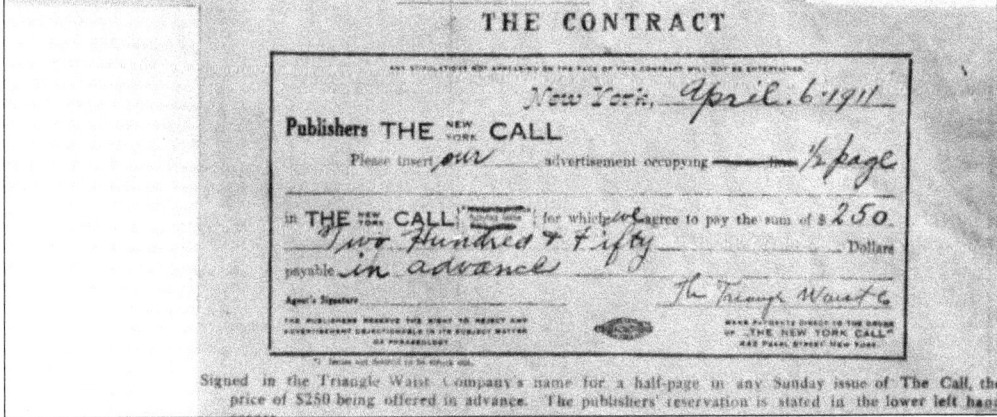

THE CONTRACT

Signed in the Triangle Waist Company's name for a half-page in any Sunday issue of The Call, the price of $250 being offered in advance. The publishers' reservation is stated in the lower left hand

This newspaper photograph is captioned: "INVESTIGATION ON ROOF OF ASCH BUILDING—From left to right Coroner Holzhauser, J. R. Rubins and C. F. Bostwick." J. Robert Rubin and Charles Bostwick were assistant district attorneys. Bostwick prosecuted Blanck and Harris.

The lantern slide caption reads: "Coroner and Jury questioning employees." The grand jury investigation led to an indictment of Max Blanck and Isaac Harris on a charge of manslaughter for causing the deaths of their employees by locking a factory door.

Mayor William J. Gaynor, fire chief Edward F. Croker, and fire commissioner Rhinelander Waldo were central to the investigation of the Triangle fire.

Chief Edward Croker (left), photographed riding with his assistant in an early motorized vehicle, attempted to modernize the New York Fire Department. In early 1911, he warned of a potential tragedy in the unsafe factories of Lower Manhattan and proposed improved fire safety laws for industry. Manufacturers claimed the proposed regulations represented government interference into commerce and the measures were defeated just months before the Triangle fire.

Robert F. Wagner was a New York State senator in 1911. He and Al Smith headed the Factory Investigating Commission, which initiated more than 30 fire safety laws. Wagner is best known for the National Labor Relations Act, which gave unions in the United States legal protection. He also sponsored bills to admit Jewish refugee children fleeing Nazism and to stop lynchings in the United States. The following excerpt from the 1912 *Preliminary Report of the New York Factory Investigating Commission* states: "This shocking loss of life aroused the community to a full sense of its responsibility. A superficial examination revealed conditions in factories and manufacturing establishments that constituted a daily menace to the lives of the thousands of working men, women and children. Lack of precautions to prevent fire, inadequate fire-escape facilities, insanitary (sic) conditions that were insidiously undermining the health of the workers were found existing everywhere. The need of a thorough and extensive investigation into the general conditions of factory life was clearly recognized."

Al Smith (standing) and Franklin Delano Roosevelt (seated) are shown here shaking hands. Roosevelt followed Smith as a progressive New York State governor. Smith ran unsuccessfully for U.S. president in 1928, but Roosevelt, promising a New Deal, won in 1932. New York progressives emerged in the aftermath of the Triangle fire and laid the basis for the New Deal. The following excerpt is from the recommendations of the *Preliminary Report of the New York Factory Investigating Commission:* "A contributing cause to the loss of life in the Triangle Waist Company fire was the lack of clear passageways leading to the fire-escapes and stairways. The employees were so crowded together, seated at tables containing machines, with chairs back to back, that when a great number of them attempted to leave at the same time there was panic and confusion."

SCENE AT FACTORY HORROR INQUIRY AND SURVIVORS WHO GAVE TESTIMONY.

This is a *New York World* portrayal of the legal inquiry into the Triangle factory fire. Survivor Sarah Cammerstein testified: "A girl hollered that the door was locked."

At the 50th anniversary commemoration ceremony of the Triangle fire, Leon Stein introduced Sarah Cammerstein to two other survivors "who fifty years earlier, almost to the hour, had lain bleeding and battered at the bottom of the elevator shaft down which each had leaped from the open ninth floor elevator door."

Kate Altermann, sketched by Artist Pugsley, as she told how Margaret Schwartz died at Triangle fire.

In her trial testimony, Kate Altermann's stated: "I noticed some one, a whole crowd around the door, and I saw Bernstein, the manager's brother, trying to open the door, and there was Margaret near him. Bernstein tried the door, he couldn't open it and then Margaret began to open the door. I take her on one side, I pushed her on the side and I said, 'Wait, I will open that door.' I tried, pulled the handle in and out, all ways—and I couldn't open it. She pushed me on the other side, got hold of the handle and then she tried. And then I saw her bending down on her knees, and her hair was loose, and the trail of her dress was a little far from her, and then a big smoke came and I couldn't see. I just know it was Margaret, and I said, 'Margaret,' and she didn't reply. I left Margaret, I turned my head on the side, and I noticed the trail of her dress and the ends of her hair begin to burn." (University of Texas Library.)

MEN INDICTED—LOCK WHICH SHUT IN GIRLS

Isaac Harris.   *Max Blanck.*

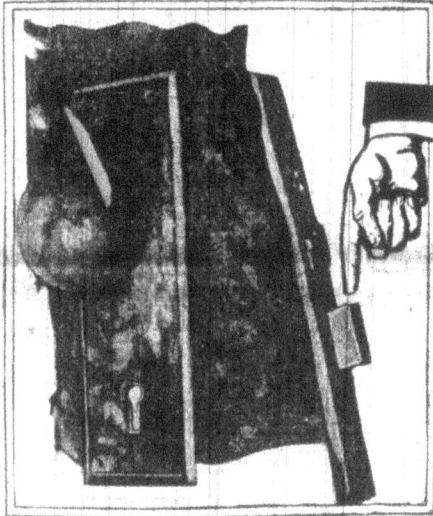

DEADLY EVIDENCE.—Charred bit of wood WITH CLOSED LOCK clinging to it. Found on Monday among debris on ninth floor of Asch Building. Was part of door of partition in floor where 400 girls were at work. Believed to have convinced the Grand Jury that girls were locked in to prevent their leaving floor till they submitted to search.

Hand points to shot bolt. As it could not have been moved since the fire because of its warped condition, the door must have been locked when the fire began.

Law Under Which Partners in Triangle Co. Were Indicted

Section 80 of the Labor law provides:

"All doors leading in or to any such factory shall be so constructed as to open outwardly, where practicable, and shall not be locked, bolted or fastened during working hours."

This newspaper article includes a photograph of a locked door from the Triangle factory, for which the owners were being indicted. The caption reads: "DEADLY EVIDENCE: Charred Bit of wood WITH CLOSED LOCK clinging to it." The Grand Jury, it was believed, found this evidence persuasive. (University of Texas Library.)

BURNED DOOR OF WAIST COMPANY SHOP; MAN WHO FOUND LOCK; ENGINEER WITNESS

CHARRED DOOR FRAME INTRODUCED *in* EVIDENCE

CONSULTING ENGINEER
JOHN D. MOORE *on* WITNESS STAND

GIUSEPPE SAVINA WHO FOUND *the* LOCK

This newspaper article appears under the headline: "BURNED DOOR OF WAIST COMPANY SHOP; MAN WHO FOUND LOCK; ENGINEER WITNESS."

90

This newspaper courtroom drawing depicts the owners of the Triangle fire at trial. Their attorney, Max Steuer was renowned, according to David Von Drehle, as "the best attorney money could buy." Affiliated with Tammany Hall, he often represented defendants with the most difficult of legal problems, and he was legendary in the success he achieved for them at trial.

MAX BLANCK   ISAAC HARRIS

STREET CROWD PURSUING MEN ON TRIAL FOR
FIRE HORROR: JUDGE EXAMINING WITNESS

JUDGE CRAIN
QUESTIONING JAMES B.
WHISKEMANN Consulting Engineer

CROWD PURSUING HARRIS and BLANCK in the STREET

Line drawings of the trial of Blanck and Harris in the *New York World* show Judge Thomas C. T. Crain questioning a witness, as well as an angry crowd pursuing the defendants in the street outside the courthouse.

MAX D. STEUER

ISAAC HARRIS   MAX BLANCK
AFTER THE VERDICT IN COURT

The broad smiles on the faces of Isaac Harris and Max Blanck are depicted here after the acquittal verdict was rendered. Based on Judge Crain's charge to the jury, they did not find the prosecution had proved beyond a reasonable doubt that the defendants *knew* that the door was locked on the day of the fire.

Max Blanck and Isaac Harris are seen here together at the time of their trial.

The strikes and rallies that took place before the Triangle fire continued to grow in militancy and size afterward. Striking garment workers are shown in these two photographs. Above shows a group of men in the street holding signs in English and Yiddish. The English sign reads "Shushansky's Workers in Essex St. Win 50 Hours $50 Treat." The photograph below shows a 1913 rally in Union Square with banners in both Yiddish and English: "United Hebrew Trades Demand Sanitary Shops" and "Freedom for All Prisoners of Lawrence Strike." Union Square, named for the intersection (union) where Broadway and Bowery Road (now Fourth Avenue) came together in the early 19th century, became a locus for demonstrations by organized workers beginning in 1882, when Labor Day originated.

This photograph of suffragettes was taken at a May Day parade.

Four

PROGRESS AND
REMEMBRANCE

Throughout the 100 years since the Triangle factory fire, the tragedy has served as a touchstone of American (as well as international) collective memory and political will. The memory of the fire has repeatedly been called upon to frame the discourses shaping many areas of social life and social identity. Unionists have invoked memory of the victims as a rallying cry in the struggles for social and economic justice. Immigrant advocates have drawn connections between the plight of the Jewish and Italian workers of 1911 and the struggles faced by succeeding waves of immigrant workers. Political leaders have directed the attention of the nation back to the tragedy during debates on important workplace safety legislation. Feminist historians have highlighted the stories of the individual workers to illustrate the discounted contributions of women in national history. In the arena of work, the New York Fire Department continues to include the fire in training curricula. The American Society of Safety Engineers, founded in response to the fire, works to avoid similar disasters. Most law schools continue to use the trial of the factory owners as an important case study, and factory workers the world over share the narrative as a reminder to remain vigilant regarding safety on the shop floor.

While the Triangle fire is considered an important part of America's national story, memory of the tragedy has alternately faded and been revived over the decades. The victims' sacrifice was fresh in the minds of many who pushed through the New Deal and reformed labor legislation in the early 20th century. In 1961, union power was at its peak in the United States and progressives used the 50th anniversary of the fire as a time to reflect back on all that had been accomplished for working people as a living memorial to the victims. As the 100-year anniversary approached, union power had precipitously declined and American workers were gripped by anxiety. Once again, unionists, activists, artists, and educators turned to the Triangle factory fire as a compelling symbol of the universal struggle for the rights and dignity of all working people.

This photograph of Frances Perkins was taken in 1911 during a Factory Investigating Commission inspection. Perkins had been having tea nearby when she heard fire engines and witnessed the fire at the nearby Asch Building. She later said, "Out of that terrible episode came a self-examination of stricken conscience in which the people of this state saw for the first time the individual worth and value of each of those 146 people who fell or were burned in that great fire . . . Moved by this sense of stricken guilt, we banded ourselves together to find a way by law to prevent this kind of disaster." (CL.)

Frances Perkins contended that the New Deal began on the day of the Triangle fire. In 1911, Perkins was working as an advocate for worker rights and as a professor of sociology at Adelphi College when she personally witnessed the horrors of the tragedy. The experience compelled her to play a leading role in the political and legislative waves of reforms that followed in the wake of the disaster. Perkins was a key member of the New York Factory Investigating Commission that successfully pushed for workplace safety laws, and after leading the New York Industrial Commission, she became Secretary of Labor under Pres. Franklin Roosevelt. As the first female presidential cabinet member, Perkins spearheaded a tremendous reform agenda, including the Social Security Act and the National Labor Relations Act of 1935. Her political acumen earned her the moniker "The Mother of the New Deal." Perkins's legislative achievements changed the lives of millions of American workers for the better and serve as a living memorial to the victims of the Triangle fire.

The Triangle fire propelled Progressivism forward in New York and paved the way for the New Deal social safety net. This photograph shows Pres. Franklin D. Roosevelt signing the Social Security Bill in 1935. Behind FDR is Secretary of Labor Frances Perkins, who saw Social Security as one of her priorities and worked tirelessly for is passage. (RC.)

The ILGWU International Headquarters building at 1710 Broadway, New York, New York, symbolized the union's rise from its ragtag beginnings to the major institution it became after the Triangle fire.

This ILGWU banner depicts labor's struggle to win its fundamental demands.

OUR UNION PIONEERS IN BRINGING EDUCATION, RECREATION, ART AND MEDICAL SCIENCE TO THE SERVICE OF LABOR

The ILGWU's "social unionism" led to the building of a broad support system for members. This ILGWU mural (around 1935) illustrates union programs such as lectures, fine arts performances, health and physical education, and outdoor recreation.

Union members Jane Hoffman, Tobey Weinberg, Ruth Goodman, and Amelia Romano broadcast an episode about the Triangle factory fire in the 1936 radio play *The Story of the ILGWU* by Florence Lasser.

Seen here in 1940 attending a performance in Madison Square Garden of the ILGWU–produced, I *Hear America Singing* are Rose Schneiderman (first row, second from left), Fiorello La Guardia (first row, third from left), David Dubinsky (first row, fourth from left), Luigi Antonini (second row, sixth from left), and many others. Schneiderman was national president of the Women's Trade Union League, La Guardia was the mayor of New York City, Dubinsky was president of the International Ladies Garment Workers Union, and Antonini was first vice president of the ILGWU, general secretary of Local 89 Italian Dressmakers Union, and president of the Italian American Labor Council. *I Hear America Singing* was broadcast on the radio coast-to-coast and was recorded by RCA Victor. According to the June 16, 1941, issue of *Time*, George Kleinsinger's "cantata" on "Whitman poems, first sung at an I.L.G.W.U. pageant, is in the vein of last year's popular, patriotalky Ballad for Americans, and sounds like a seller."

The ILGWU–produced play *Pins and Needles* explored historical and current events from a union perspective. The play, performed by union workers, proved so popular that it moved to Broadway's Windsor Theater. This was the first time a play produced by a group of theatrical amateurs became a successful Broadway show.

First Lady Eleanor Roosevelt (left), labor activist Rose Schneiderman (center), and ILGWU president David Dubinsky (right) attend a 1938 performance of the ILGWU–produced *Pins and Needles*.

Eleanor Roosevelt and
Pres. John F. Kennedy attend
the dedication of the ILGWU
cooperative housing project in
New York City in 1962. The union-
built, affordable housing made
available to members represented
one of the greatest achievements
of ILGWU social unionism.

The ILGWU demonstrated continued dedication to worker safety by parading a fire truck on
Labor Day. The banner reads, "ILGWU Fire Wardens Cooperate With N.Y. Fire Department In
Saving Lives Through Fire Prevention."

Large crowds gather at the site of the Triangle factory fire for the 50th anniversary commemoration ceremony on March 25, 1961. A New York City fire truck raises a ladder towards the windows above but does not extend it beyond the sixth floor, the limit that the longest fire ladder could reach in 1911.

New York City firemen salute at the site of the Triangle factory fire during the 50th anniversary commemoration of the tragedy.

Frances Perkins (left) and Eleanor Roosevelt (right) sat together at the 50th anniversary commemoration of the Triangle fire. These two distinguished women were at the forefront of the historic movement to secure basic human rights for working people. Frances Perkins was a witness to the Triangle fire and became a successful champion of workplace safety and workers' rights, first in New York State and then as FDR's Secretary of Labor. She championed New Deal labor legislation that safeguarded American workers and facilitated unionization. Eleanor Roosevelt became U.S. delegate to the UN General Assembly, where her committee created the Universal Declaration of Human Rights, for which achievement President Truman called her "The First Lady of the World." At the 50th anniversary ceremony, Frances Perkins said of the Triangle workers, "They did not die in vain, and we will never forget them."

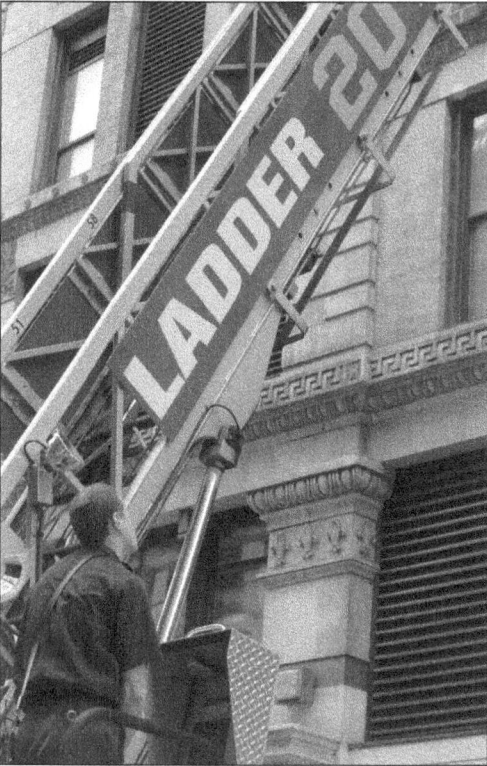

New York City firemen participate in the 99th anniversary commemoration of the fire. Ladder 20 was the first ladder company to arrive at the burning Triangle factory, and each year Ladder 20 raises a ladder only to the sixth floor of the building to dramatically illustrate the tragic inadequacy of the firefighting equipment available in 1911. (Robert Domingo, FDNY.)

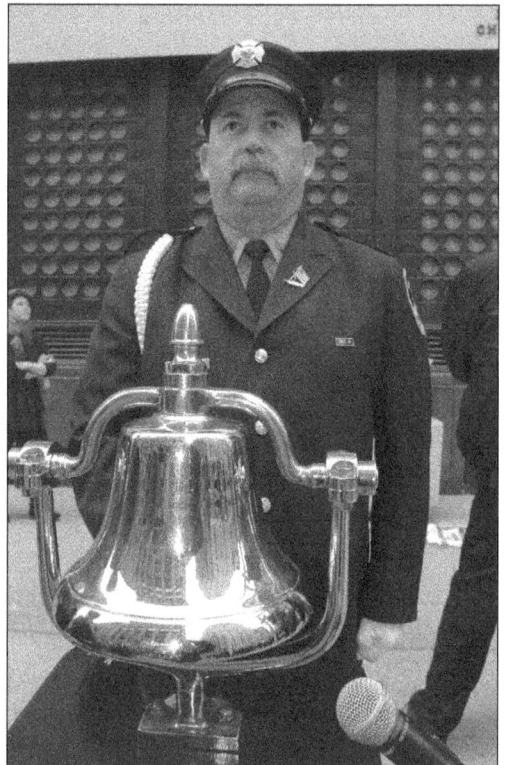

This photograph was taken at the 99th anniversary commemoration of the Triangle fire. At these ceremonies, a New York City fireman rings a bell as each victim's name is called. (Robert Domingo, FDNY.)

The New York City Labor Chorus sings while New York City public school children look on at the 99th anniversary commemoration. (Robert Domingo, FDNY.)

At the 99th anniversary commemoration of the Triangle fire, a New York City public school teacher assists students as they lay flowers in memory of each of the victims. (Robert Domingo, FDNY.)

New York City–based artist Ruth Sergel conceived and organized the Chalk Project, a participatory public art project that on each anniversary of the tragedy encourages individuals or groups to inscribe in chalk the names of Triangle fire victims on the sidewalks outside the homes where they lived. (Rob Linné.)

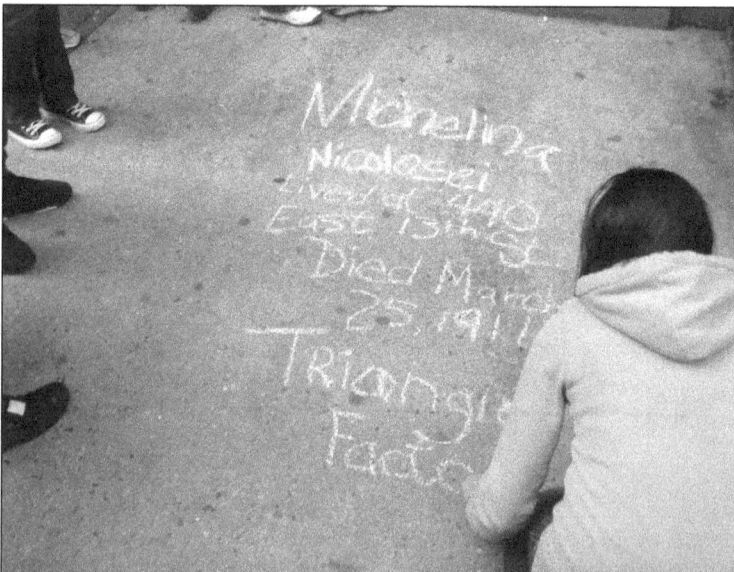

On the 99th anniversary, a New York City public school student chalked outside the home of fire victim Michelina Nicolosei, who lived in the East Village. The inscription reads, "Michelina Nicolosei Lived at 440 East 13th St. Died March 25, 1911, in the Triangle Factory." (Rob Linné.)

Researcher Michael Hirsch has documented all the Triangle fire victims' grave sites. Hirsch also works to clean and repair the grave sites that have fallen into disrepair. In winter 2010, Hirsch coordinated a group, including Adelphi University faculty and students, in cleaning and repairing Rose Schneiderman's grave at Maimonides Cemetery in Elmont, Long Island. In this photograph, Michael Hirsch is removing a tree stump as Mark Bannick looks on. (Rob Linné.)

Michael Hirsch has organized the restoration of Triangle fire victims' grave sites. At the dedication of a new gravestone for Jacob Bernstein on March 29, 2010, in Mount Richmond Cemetery on Staten Island, Rabbi Peter Schweitzer said, "On behalf of Jacob Bernstein's family, and on behalf of the larger human family who are all mourners of this event, we consecrate this stone as a sign of our remembrance, devotion and everlasting bond." (Rob Linné.)

As the centennial of the fire approached, many artists and educators conceived projects to commemorate the victims through performances, art exhibitions, teach-ins, lectures, and symposia. New York City–based writer and actress LuLu Lolo wrote *Soliloquy for a Seamstress*, based on the lives of the Saracino sisters, Italian immigrants who died in the fire. (LuLu LoLo.)

Artists and writers have created a tremendous body of work in remembrance of the Triangle fire, including murals, paintings, songs, plays, radio plays, films, poems, novels, and adolescent and children's literature. With the publication of *The Triangle Shirtwaist Fire* in 2006, Capstone Press retold the story in the contemporary idiom of the graphic novel.

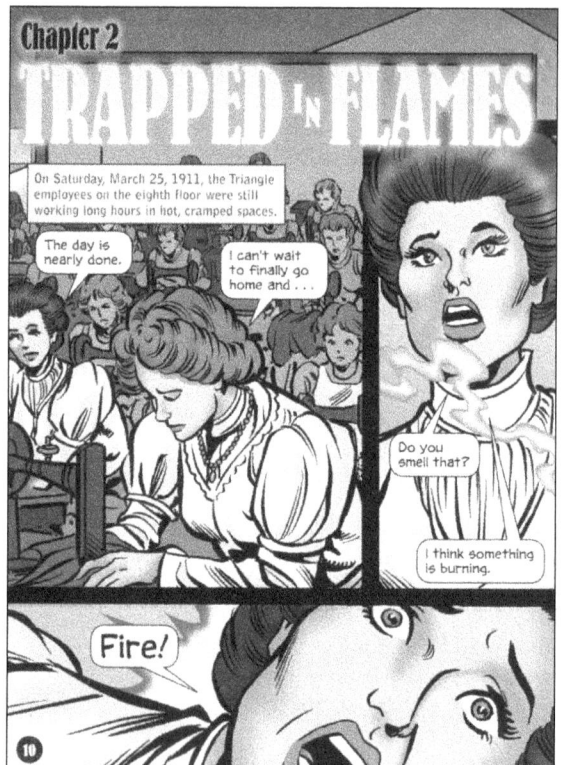

Five

TRIANGLE: REMEMBERING THE FIRE, A DOCUMENTARY FILM BY HBO

Sheila Nevins, the longtime head of nonfiction programming at HBO, asked the producers at Blowback Productions to make a film about the economy, which had not yet crashed in the spring of 2007, but was showing signs of a widening chasm between rich and poor. After doing a significant amount of research, they pitched various ways into the story—hedge funds, the new super rich, profiling an entire city. She suggested looking at the issue through the story of the garment industry. They were taken aback! What could she possibly be thinking?! Was there any garment industry left in America? Hadn't it all been outsourced years ago? How were the producers going to tell this story? She just smiled and said, "You'll figure it out." They ended up calling it *Schmatta: Rags to Riches to Rags*, and it was about the rise and fall of the garment industry. It became one of the most requested documentary films ever done for HBO.

Blowback laid out the story chronologically, starting with immigration and following the history through the Triangle fire, the labor movement, and the ultimate outsourcing of the production side of the industry. As they were making the film, Sheila revealed that she may have had a great-aunt Celia who died in the fire. A list of the victims showed that she did indeed work at the factory and that she had a fractured skull, indicating that she had jumped from the building. Sheila was so moved that she wrote a letter to Celia, which is included in this book. She also asked the producers to make an entire film just about the Triangle fire for the 100th anniversary in 2011. Her family connection inspired them to find other descendents to tell the story of the fire. They spoke with relatives of the victims, the owners, a fireman, Al Smith, and the attorney who successfully defended the company.

The producers began to feel that Celia's spirit, from the beginning, had been moving them to bring the story back to life and to give a voice to those people who suffered and died, to remember that they were individuals, not just a group of nameless workers, and to caution the group to see that the fire is still burning in workplaces where owners and government put money over the well-being and safety of employees.

The production team was Marc Levin, Daphne Pinkerson, Nancy Abraham, Michael Hirsch, Richard Lowe, John Hazard, Kara Rozansky, Chris Walker, and Justin Sirizzotti.

Following are excerpts from the film.

Rose Alter, a bookkeeper, survived the fire. Her granddaughter, Amy Kolen, said, "My grandmother says that we heard the word 'fire' and within 10 minutes we were surrounded on all four sides by flames. The place just went up. It was an inferno." (Amy Kolen.)

Rosie Weiner, seen here, died in the fire; her sister, Katie, survived. Their grandniece Suzanne Pred Bass said, "When the fire broke out, Katie told me she was actually with Rosie and then lost her in the smoke. I think Rosie may have gone back to look for Katie, who was the older sibling. Rosie never made it out." (Suzanne Pred Bass.)

New York City fireman Andrew Ott was with Ladder Company 20. His grandson, fire marshal Raymond Ott, said, "My grandfather was with the first hook and ladder company to arrive on the scene that day. He saw women jumping out of the windows holding their pocketbooks. I was at 9/11, watching the people jump. It must have been very similar to what my grandfather saw that day." (Raymond Ott.)

Joseph Zito was one the elevator operators. His great-great grandson, Dennis Clancey, said, "He was going into the fire to save those people that he knew would die if he wasn't able to get back up there. He saved over 100 people that day." (Dennis Clancey.)

Seen here are Catherine Maltese (left) and her daughters Lucia and Rosaria (below). Vincent Maltese said, "My grandmother was a sewing machine operator, Lucia, 18, was an operator just beginning, and Rosaria, 14, was a floor girl who used to bring the work to the people who were sewing. They worked on the 9th floor and they all died that day." (Vincent Maltese.)

This image of Fannie Lansner (top row, left) was published in the *New York Evening Telegram* on Monday March 27, 1911. Her grandniece, Erica Lansner, said, "Fannie, in her role as supervisor, tried to usher as many people as she could into the elevator. She remained a beacon of calmness while there was so much panic around her. She expected the elevator to come back and get her. It had already made eight or nine trips. But it was not possible and she was forced to jump out of the window to her death."

Survivor Sylvia Reigler was an 18-year-old sewing machine operator. Her great-granddaughter, Stacey Silverstein, said, "Her good friend Rose Feibisch ran in a panic, screaming and pulling her towards the window. But even as a child Sylvia had a great fear of heights so she broke free and ran the opposite way. She said, 'I turned back into the shop. Rose Feibisch, my beautiful, dear friend, jumped from a window.'" (Stacey Silverstein.)

Rose Oringer jumped to her death. Her cousin, Leigh Benin, said, "People forget the Triangle fire at their peril. This whole movement against regulation of industry—if people want to know what would deregulated industry look like, look at the bodies on the sidewalk outside the Triangle building." (Philip Maier.)

Susan Harris, granddaughter of Triangle Waist Company co-owner Max Blanck, is seen here at the annual commemoration of the Triangle fire looking at a photograph of the burned ninth floor. "My grandfather wanted to be successful. He wanted to have one of the bigger and better businesses," she said. (Robert Domingo, FDNY.)

Six

ECHOES

The horrors of the Triangle factory fire inspired a series of workplace safety and fire prevention laws. Labor laws were reformed to give unions greater power to organize in order to protect the interests of workers and serve as a check on unscrupulous factory owners. Yet, reminders of the Triangle factory fire appear again and again in stories with eerily similar trajectories of unsafe work environments leading to tragic deaths. During the year leading up to the 100th anniversary of the Triangle factory fire, two workplace disasters in particular captured the nation's attention. An explosion at the Upper Big Branch coal mine in West Virginia took 29 lives. Massey Energy, the corporate mine owner, had been cited repeatedly for safety violations while using political contributions to lobby for less stringent safety standards and enforcement. In summer 2010, British Petroleum's Deepwater Horizon oil rig exploded, killing 11 workers, injuring 17 others, and leaking millions of gallons of oil into the ecologically fragile Gulf of Mexico in the worst environmental disaster in U.S. history. British Petroleum had been cited numerous times for safety violations as well as previous accidents and explosions in the Gulf area.

Many more large-scale workplace disasters occur in developing countries as manufacturers continue to move operations overseas to exploit cheap labor and minimal safety standards. A 2010 late night fire at the Garib and Garib factory in Bangladesh that manufactures clothes for international retailer H&M killed at least 21 workers, mostly women, and injured over 50. The workers had no route of escape, and what fire safety equipment was found at the site proved worthless. This fire followed a string of disasters at factory deathtraps across southeast Asia that have taken the lives of thousands of workers.

These tragedies illustrate the need to view the Triangle factory fire from the perspective of the contemporary globalized economy. Triangle factory–like conditions have been outsourced to the developing world, and American workers cannot ignore the consequences. Today's labor movement necessarily encompasses a global perspective. American garment unions fight to improve working conditions overseas and immigrant rights at home. Economic justice campaigns and curricula focus on child labor and unsafe factories producing American apparel popular with youth. In all these campaigns for human rights, the Triangle factory fire remains a powerful symbol in the struggle for social justice.

The Garment Worker by Judith Weller was dedicated in 1984. The 8-foot-high bronze sculpture, located at 555 Seventh Avenue (between Thirty-ninth and Fortieth Streets) in New York City, is a permanent public statue that was commissioned by the ILGWU and the Public Art Fund of New York City. (Rob Linné.)

The once mighty garment center in New York City has suffered from the outsourcing of labor, dwindling from hundreds of thousands of jobs to a few thousand by 2010. To save what remains of garment manufacturing, New York's fashion industry joined forces with labor and city universities to lobby government to keep garment jobs in New York. Save the Garment Center organized this rally in spring 2010. (Rob Linné.)

118

Fannia Cohn, Rose Schneiderman, and others commemorate the 50th anniversary of the Uprising of the 20,000 at Cooper Union.

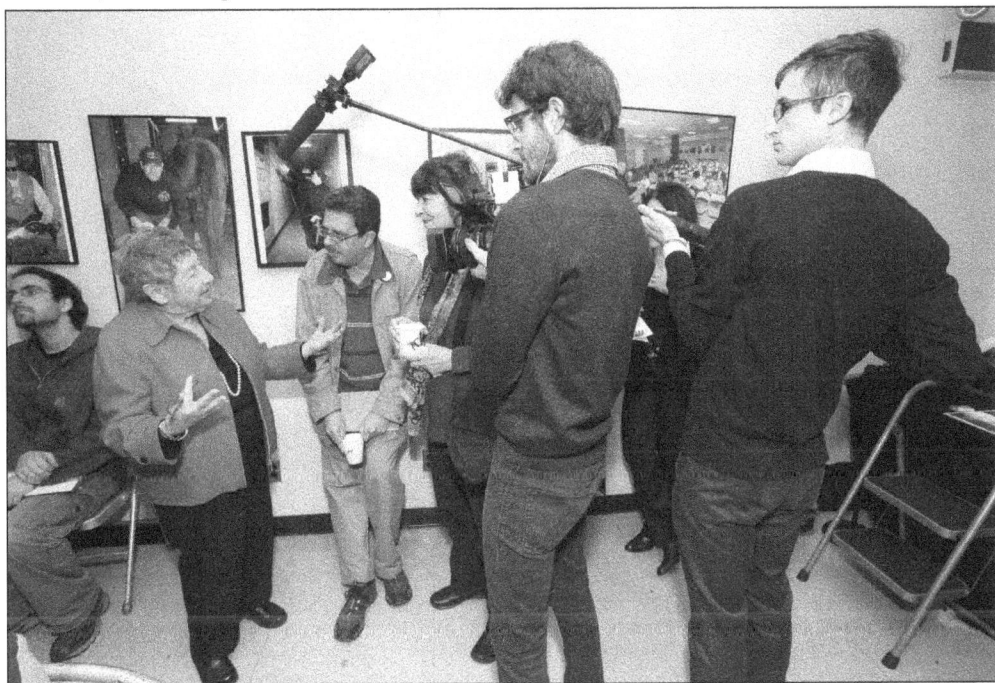

The Education and Labor Collaborative and Adelphi University organized a 100th anniversary commemoration of the Uprising of the 20,000. Rita Margules, daughter of Clara Lemlich, was interviewed by Blowback Productions/HBO Documentary Films after speaking to the overflow audience. (Rob Linné.)

The Union of Needletrades, Industrial, and Textile Employees (UNITE), immediate successor of the ILGWU, organized a large Christmas demonstration against sweatshops outside of a Guess store in New York City. Signs displayed photographs of sweatshop workers with text reading, "There are no holidays in a sweatshop." (Workers United.)

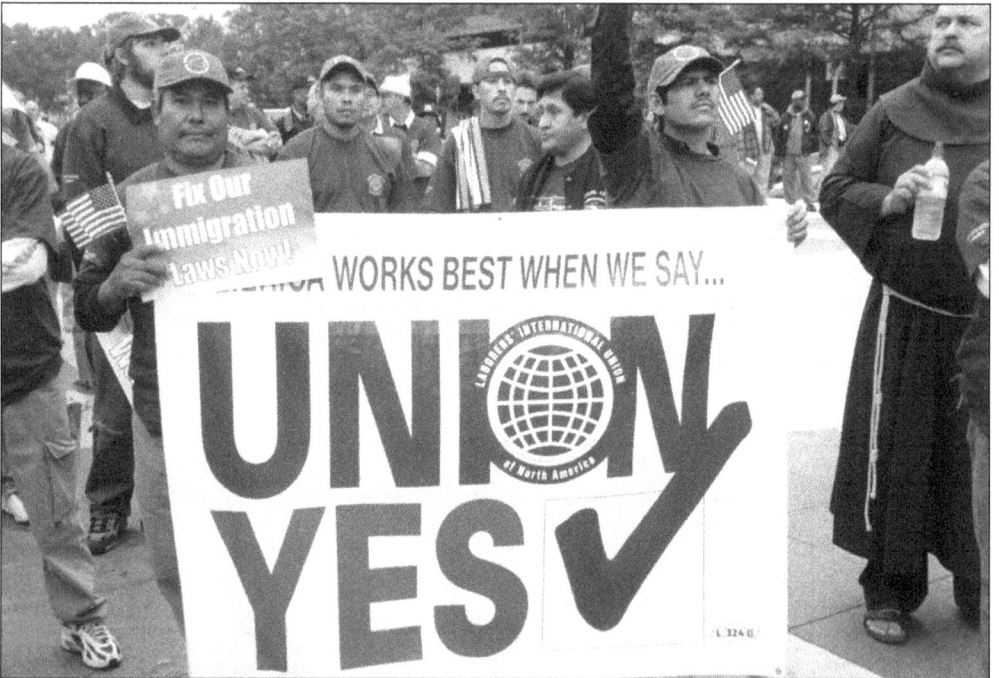

Members of the Laborers' International Union of North America march for union solidarity and call attention to contemporary immigrant issues. The exploitation of immigrant labor has continued as a fact of life in the American workplace, mirroring the conditions of immigrants who struggled for dignity and decent conditions in 1911. (Workers United.)

UNITE organized a large demonstration outside a Niketown store in New York City to protest sweatshop conditions in overseas factories. The multilingual signs illustrate the fact that Nike was paying workers as little as 13¢ an hour to make the shoes sold by this very profitable company. (Workers United.)

Children of ILGWU members protest for safer working conditions for their parents and all workers. These young demonstrators carry signs displaying photographs of the burned interior of the Triangle factory with text demanding, "No more Triangle fires."

A temporary memorial, including the words "Remember the Triangle Fire" inscribed in chalk, was created at the site of the fire during the 99th commemoration ceremony. (Robert Domingo, FDNY.)

123

Listed below are the given name, surname, age, and country of origin of each victim of the Triangle factory fire. This list was provided by Michael Hirsch.

Lizzie Adler, 24, Romania
Anna Altman, 16, Russia
Annina Ardito, 25, Italy
Rose Bassino, 31, Italy
Vincenza Benanti, 22, Italy
Yetta Berger, 18, Austria
Essie Bernstein, 19, Russia
Jacob Bernstein, 38, Russia
Morris Bernstein, 19, Russia
Gussie Bierman, 22, Russia
Vincenza Billota, 16, Italy
Abraham Binowitz, 30, Russia
Rosie Brenman, 23, Russia
Sarah Brenman, 17, Russia
Ida Brodsky, 15, Russia
Sarah Brodsky, 21, Russia
Ada Brooks, 18, United States
Laura Brunetti, 17, Italy
Josephine Cammarata, 17, Italy
Francesca Caputo, 17, Italy
Josephine Carlisi, 31, Italy
Albina Caruso, 20, United States
Annie Ciminello, 36, Italy
Rosina Cirrito, 18, Italy
Anna Cohen, 25, Russia
Annie Colletti, 30, Italy
Sarah Cooper, 16, Russia
Michelina Cordiano, 25, Italy
Bessie Dashefsky, 25, Russia
Josie Del Castillo, 21, Italy
Clara Dockman, 19, Russia
Kalman Donick, 24, Russia
Celia Eisenberg, 17, Russia
Dora Evans, 18, Russia
Rebecca Feibisch, 20, Romania
Yetta Fichtenholtz, 18, Russia
Daisy Lopez Fitze, 26, Jamaica
Mary Floresta, 26, Italy
Max Florin, 23, Russia
Jennie Franco, 16, United States
Rose Friedman, 18, Russia
Diana Gerjuoy, 18, Russia
Molly Gerstein, 17, Russia
Catherine Giannattasio, 22, Italy
Celia Gitlin, 17, Russia
Esther Goldstein, 20, Russia
Lena Goldstein, 22, Russia
Mary Goldstein, 18, Russia

Yetta Goldstein, 20, Russia
Rosie Grasso, 16 Italy
Bertha Greb, 25, United States
Rachel Grossman, 18, Romania
Mary Herman, 40, Austria
Esther Hochfeld, 21, Russia
Fannie Hollander, 18, Austria
Pauline Horowitz, 19, Russia
Ida Jukofsky, 19, Russia
Ida Kanowitz, 18, Russia
Tessie Kaplan, 18, Russia
Beckie Kessler, 19, Russia
Jacob Klein, 23, Russia
Beckie Koppelman, 16, Russia
Bertha Kula, 19, Austria
Tillie Kupferschmidt, 16, Austria
Benjamin Kurtz, 19, Russia
Annie L'Abbate, 16, Italy
Fannie Lansner, 21, Russia
Maria Giuseppa Lauletti, 33, Italy
Jennie Lederman, 21, Russia
Max Lehrer, 18, Austria
Sam Lehrer, 19, Austria
Kate Leone, 14, United States
Mary Leventhal, 22, United States
Jennie Levin, 19, Russia
Pauline Levine, 19, Russia
Nettie Liebowitz, 23, Romania
Rose Liermark, 19, Russia
Bettina Maiale, 18, Italy
Frances Maiale, 21, Italy
Catherine Maltese, 39, Italy
Lucia Maltese, 20, Italy
Rosaria Maltese, 14, Italy
Maria Manara, 27, Italy
Rose Mankofsky, 22, Russia
Rose Mehl, 15, United States
Yetta Meyers, 19, Russia
Gaetana Midolo, 16, Italy
Annie Miller, 16, Austria
Beckie Neubauer, 19, Austria
Annie Nicholas, 18, Russia
Michelina Nicolosci, 21, Italy
Sadie Nussbaum, 18, United States
Julia Oberstein, 19, United States
Rose Oringer, 19, Austria
Beckie Ostrovsky, 20, Russia
Annie Pack, 18, Austria

Provindenza Panno, 43, Italy
Antonietta Pasqualicchio, 16, Italy
Ida Pearl, 20, Russia
Jennie Pildescu, 18, Romania
Vincenza Pinelli, 30, Italy
Emilia Prato, 21, United States
Concetta Prestifilippo, 22, Italy
Beckie Reines, 18, Russia
Fannie Rosen, 21, Russia
Israel Rosen, 17, Russia
Julia Rosen, 35, Russia
Louis Rosen, 33, Russia
Yetta Rosenbaum, 22, Russia
Jennie Rosenberg, 21, Russia
Gussie Rosenfeld, 22, Russia
Nettie Rosenthal, 21, Russia
Emma Rothstein, 22, Russia
Theodore Rotner, 22, Russia
Sarah Sabasowitz, 17, Russia
Santina Salemi, 24, Italy
Sarafina Saracino, 25, Italy
Teresina Saracino, 20, Italy
Gussie Schiffman, 18, Russia
Theresa Schmidt, 32, Austria
Ethel Schneider, 20, Russia
Violet Schochet, 21, Austria
Golda Schpunt, 19, Russia
Margaret Schwartz, 24, Hungary
Jacob Seltzer, 33, Russia
Rosie Shapiro, 17, Russia
Ben Sklover, 25, Russia
Rose Sorkin, 18, Russia
Annie Starr, 30, Russia
Jennie Stein, 18, Russia
Jennie Stellino, 16, Italy
Jennie Stiglitz, 22, Austria
Sam Taback, 20, Russia
Clotilde Terranova, 22, Italy
Isabella Tortorelli, 17, Italy
Meyer Uttal, 23, Russia
Catherine Uzzo, 22, Italy
Frieda Velakofsky, 20, Russia
Bessie Viviano, 15, Italy
Rosie Weiner, 20, Russia
Sarah Weintraub, 17, Austria
Tessie Weisner, 21, Austria
Dora Welfowitz, 21, Russia
Bertha Wendroff, 18, Russia
Joseph Wilson, 22, Russia
Sonia Wisotsky, 17, Russia

SELECTED BIBLIOGRAPHY

Argersinger, Jo Ann E. *The Triangle Fire: A Brief History with Documents (The Bedford Series in History and Culture)*, 2009.

Downey, Kirstin. *The Woman Behind the New Deal: The Life of Frances Perkins, FDR's Secretary of Labor and His Moral Conscience*. New York: Doubleday, 2009.

Greenwald, Richard A. *The Triangle Fire, the Protocols of Peace, and Industrial Democracy in Progressive Era New York*. Philadelphia: Temple University Press, 2005.

Orleck, Annelise. *Common Sense and a Little Fire: Women and Working-Class Politics in the United States, 1900–1965*. Chapel Hill, NC: University of North Carolina Press, 1995.

Stein, Leon, ed. *Out of the Sweatshop: The Struggle for Industrial Democracy*. New York: Quadrangle/New York Times Book Company, 1977.

———. *The Triangle Fire*. Ithaca, New York: Cornell University Press, 2001.

Todd, Ellen Wiley. "Remembering the Unknowns: The Longman Memorial and the 1911 Triangle Shirtwaist Fire." *American Art* 23,3 (Fall 2009). 60–80.

Tyler, Gus. *Look for the Union Label: A History of the International Ladies Garment Workers Union*. New York: M. E. Sharpe, 1995.

Von Drehle, David. *Triangle: The Fire That Changed America*. New York: Atlantic Monthly Press, 2003.

The Kheel Center for Labor-Management Documentation and Archives at Cornell University, in cooperation with the Union of Needletrades, Industrial, and Textile Employees (UNITE, now Workers United), in 1998 created an online exhibit Web site, www.ilr.cornell.edu/trianglefire, which is continually updated and contains an extensive bibliography that includes archive sources, fiction, poetry, videos, juvenile literature, and instructional materials.

ABOUT THE
ORGANIZATIONS

THE EDUCATION AND LABOR COLLABORATIVE

The Education and Labor Collaborative works to organize unionists and educators with the goal of addressing the absence of labor history and education in contemporary U.S. schools. Participants represent a broad coalition, including union educators and organizers, teachers and teacher educators, university students and academics. The Education and Labor Collaborative has organized forums and teaching institutes, including the 100-year anniversary commemoration of the "Uprising of the 20,000," "Teaching the New New Deal," and "Teaching the Triangle Factory Fire." Publications inspired by the organization's mission include: *Organizing the Curriculum: Perspectives on Teaching the US Labor Movement*, edited by Rob Linné, Leigh Benin, and Andi Sosin. The Education and Labor Collaborative is housed at Adelphi University.

INTERNATIONAL LADIES' GARMENT WORKERS' UNION (ILGWU, NOW WORKERS UNITED)

Workers United, SEIU is a merger of the former ILGWU and the Amalgamated Textile Workers Union. The ILGWU was founded in 1900 by immigrant workers in New York City's garment industry. In 1909, ILGWU Local 25 attempted to organize the Triangle Shirtwaist Company, but the owners denied the union recognition. On March 25, 1911, fire swept the factory killing 146 workers who died senseless deaths because of unsafe working conditions. The tragedy strengthened workers' resolve to organize and led to transformational labor law reform and workplace safety legislation. The ILGWU grew into one of the most important labor unions in the United States and organized many historically important actions. The outsourcing of garment manufacturing to low-wage labor markets abroad over the past 50 years has severely reduced the union's membership. The ILGWU's history of "social unionism" includes the nation's first union health center, educational and cultural programs, housing projects, an affordable recreational facility, a bilingual childcare center, scholarship funds, and assistance for immigrant workers seeking U.S. citizenship.

BLOWBACK PRODUCTIONS AND HBO DOCUMENTARY FILMS

Blowback Productions was created by Marc Levin in 1988. He and his producing partner, Daphne Pinkerson, have made over 20 films that have won Emmys, DuPonts, Cable Aces, and numerous other awards and accolades. They have told powerful real stories in a unique authentic style. HBO Documentary Films has produced many influential and award-winning documentary films, including *Schmatta: From Rags to Riches to Rags* (2009), which documents the rise and fall of New York City's garment industry as a case study of the deindustrialization of the United States. *Triangle: Remembering the Fire* was produced for the Triangle fire centennial.

Visit us at
arcadiapublishing.com

www.ingramcontent.com/pod-product-compliance
Lightning Source LLC
Chambersburg PA
CBHW050706110426
42813CB00007B/2098